BALLPARK

RECIPES INSPIRED BY
America's Baseball Stadiums

★ BY ★

Katrina Jorgensen

CAPSTONE YOUNG READERS
a Capstone imprint

Sections

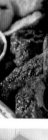

Introduction

In 1908, songwriter Jack Norworth penned "Take Me Out to the Ball Game," and his lyrics "buy me some peanuts and cracker jack" solidified the relationship between food and baseball. More than one hundred years later, his song remains the game's seventh-inning anthem, and food remains indelibly linked with America's Greatest Pastime. Little has changed — except the menus!

Today, Major League Baseball stadiums across the United States and Canada offer a dizzying array of edible options. Vendor chants of "Peanuts! Get your peanuts here!" still echo across the hallowed grounds of Fenway Park, Wrigley Field, and Dodger Stadium. But baseball's most memorable sounds and smells — like the crack of a bat or the scent of fresh-cut grass — now include the sizzle of a New York strip, the snap of a Chicago Dog, and the sweet, smoky aromas of Kansas City barbecue and Cincinnati-style chili.

From the Atlantic to the Pacific, Major League ballparks are as unique — in both culture and cuisine — as the thirty cities and states they represent. Pittsburgh's PNC Park offers views of a bustling East Coast city, while St. Louis's Busch Stadium looks out on the Gateway to the West. The retractable roof at Milwaukee's Miller Park shelters poor-weather fans through postseason play, while San Diego's Petco Park showcases a season full of seventy-and-sunny.

Like the stadiums themselves, *Sports Illustrated KIDS Ballpark Eats* delivers a taste of each city's local flavor and a chance for chefs and sports fans, young and old, to experience a culinary road trip at home. So step up to the plate and take a crack at one of these diamond dishes, perfect for any seventh-inning stretch.

American League

East Division

Central Division

West Division

BAL

Baltimore Orioles Baseball Club

ORIOLE PARK
AT CAMDEN YARDS

LOCATION
Baltimore, Maryland
OPENED
1992
CAPACITY
45,971
NICKNAMES
The Yard
Birdland
The House That Cal Built

Oriole Park at Camden Yards is home to the Baltimore Orioles. Opening on April 6, 1992, the stadium became the first of the so-called "retro" ballparks. In contrast to large, multipurpose stadiums, such as the Orioles's former Memorial Stadium, the throwback features of Camden Yards reminded fans of ballparks of yesteryear: downtown location, limited capacity, and amazing views. Fans at Camden Yards have witnessed many great moments in baseball history, but perhaps none greater than Cal Ripken Jr.'s record-setting 2,131st consecutive game on September 6, 1995. In fact, the ballpark itself is sometimes referred to as "The House that Cal Built."

MARYLAND CRAB CAKE SLIDERS

with TARTAR SAUCE & BERRY SPRITZER

Located in downtown Baltimore, Maryland, Camden Yards sits only miles away from the salty waters of Chesapeake Bay. For generations, the bay has inspired and supported the local cuisine, including Baltimore's favorite treat: crab cakes. These crisp, buttery patties of crabmeat are a perfect seventh-inning snack for any baseball fan.

MARYLAND CRAB CAKE SLIDERS

PREP 15 MINUTES

COOK 10 MINUTES

MAKES 8 SLIDERS

INGREDIENTS

◇	¼ bunch	flat-leaf parsley
◇	4	green onions
◇	12 ounces	lump crabmeat, drained
◇	½ cup	mayonnaise
◇	2	eggs
◇	1 cup	panko bread crumbs
◇	1 teaspoon	seafood seasoning
◇	¼ teaspoon	salt
◇	½ teaspoon	ground black pepper
◇	2 tablespoons	oil, for frying
◇	8	slider buns
◇	8 leaves	lettuce

1. Chop parsley and green onion finely and place in a mixing bowl.

2. Add crabmeat, mayonnaise, eggs, bread crumbs, seafood seasoning, salt, and black pepper. Mix lightly with a fork until combined.

3. Separate the crab cake mix into 8 equal pieces. Shape into patties.

4. Place the oil in a nonstick skillet and put on a stove burner. Set on medium heat.

5. Carefully place the patties in the hot pan, about ½-inch apart. You may have to work in batches.

6. Cook one side for 4 minutes, and then flip the cakes over with tongs and fry an additional 4 minutes.

7. Remove the finished crab cakes from the pan.

8. To assemble the sliders, split the slider buns, place a crab cake on the bottom half, followed by a leaf of lettuce. Spread 1 tablespoon of tartar sauce on the top half and place on top of the lettuce. Serve immediately.

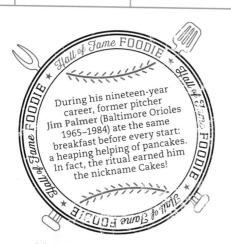

Hall of Fame FOODIE

During his nineteen-year career, former pitcher Jim Palmer (Baltimore Orioles 1965–1984) ate the same breakfast before every start: a heaping helping of pancakes. In fact, the ritual earned him the nickname Cakes!

TARTAR SAUCE

PREP	COOK	MAKES
5	**0**	**½**
MINUTES	MINUTES	CUP

INGREDIENTS

◇	2	green onions
◇	½ cup	mayonnaise
◇	2 tablespoons	sweet pickle relish
◇	1 teaspoon	Dijon mustard
◇	1 teaspoon	lemon juice
◇	½ teaspoon	salt
◇	¼ teaspoon	ground black pepper
◇		
◇		

1 Chop the green onions finely and add to a mixing bowl.

2 Add remaining ingredients and stir to combine.

3 Serve on Maryland Crab Cake Sliders. Store leftovers in refrigerator for up to 3 days.

BERRY SPRITZER

PREP	COOK	MAKES
5	**0**	**2**
MINUTES	MINUTES	QUARTS

INGREDIENTS

◇	1 quart	berry juice
◇	1 quart	sparkling water
◇	handful of each	strawberries
◇		raspberries
◇		blueberries

1 Combine the berry juice and sparkling water in a pitcher. Stir lightly to combine.

2 Pour into glasses with several strawberries, raspberries, and blueberries for garnish.

BOS

FENWAY PARK

LOCATION
Boston, Massachusetts
OPENED
1912
CAPACITY
37,673
NICKNAMES
The Cathedral of Boston
America's Most Beloved Ballpark

Built in 1912, Fenway Park holds the title as the oldest ballpark in Major League Baseball. The stadium was built in an area of Boston called "The Fens," or "Fenway," thus the name. But the park has changed a lot over the years. The Green Monster, a towering 37-foot-tall wall in left field, was added in 1934. The stands are now concrete instead of the original wood. Still, stepping into Fenway Park is like traveling back in baseball history. Greats like Babe Ruth and Ted Williams once called it home. And the Red Sox have won eight World Series titles — starting with one the year Fenway Park opened — in their more than 100-year history.

BOSTON FRANK

with BAKED BEANS & MINI BOSTON CREAM PIES

Located on the Atlantic Coast, Boston, Massachusetts is no stranger to seafood, and Fenway fans welcome it with open mouths. From New England eats like lobster rolls and clam chowder to oysters and sushi, the oceanic options can feed a sell-out crowd. But at the league's oldest park, classics are king, and this simple, snappy frankfurter is top dog.

BOSTON FRANK

PREP	COOK	MAKES
5	**5**	**4**
MINUTES	MINUTES	DOGS

	INGREDIENTS	
◇	4	hot dogs
◇	½ cup	sweet pickle relish
◇	1	small onion
◇	4	hot dog buns*
◇	to taste	spicy yellow mustard
◇		
◇	* Typically served on New England-style	
◇	rolls (as shown). These tear-apart	
◇	flat-sided rolls are often buttered and	
◇	grilled for added flavor. However, standard	
◇	hot dogs buns can also be used.	

1 In a skillet, add 3 cups of water and place hot dogs in the water. Turn the heat on stove to medium and bring to a simmer. Cook for 5 minutes.

2 While the hot dogs are simmering, dice the onion. Set aside.

3 When the hot dogs are done, remove from the pan with tongs and place in the hot dog buns.

4 Spread 2 tablespoons of the sweet pickle relish on each hot dog.

5 Add as much spicy yellow mustard to your liking, followed by a sprinkling of the chopped onions. Serve immediately.

FRANK FACTS:

In 1893, Chris von der Ahe, owner of the St. Louis Browns Major League baseball team, served the first ballpark sausage.

In April 1901, a vendor at the New York Polo Grounds sold "dachshund sausages," which *New York Journal* cartoonist Tad Dorgan later described as "hot dogs."

In 2015, the National Hot Dog and Sausage Council estimated that more than 18.5 million hot dogs and sausages were served at Major League ballparks. That's enough hot dogs to stretch from Los Angeles's Dodger Stadium to Wrigley Field in Chicago, Illinois!

Today, each vendor at a Major League ballpark sells approximately 150 hot dogs per game, or about 10,000–12,000 hot dogs per season!

National Hot Dog Day, an annual celebration of all things frankfurter, is held each year on the third Saturday in July.

BAKED BEANS

PREP	COOK	MAKES
10	**1**	**4–6**
MINUTES	HOUR	SERVINGS

	INGREDIENTS	
◇	1 tablespoon	butter
◇	1	small onion
◇	3 slices	thick-cut bacon
◇	1/4 cup	barbecue sauce
◇	2 tablespoons	brown sugar
◇	1 teaspoon	dry mustard
◇	2 16-ounce cans	pork and beans

1 Preheat oven to 350°F.

2 Chop the onion finely and set aside.

3 Cube the bacon into ½-inch pieces and set aside.

4 In a large sauté pan, heat the butter over medium heat.

5 Add the bacon and onion to the sauté pan. Sauté for about 5 minutes or until the onions have softened slightly. Stir in the remaining ingredients.

6 Pour the contents of the sauté pan into the baking dish.

7 Bake in the oven for about one hour and serve hot.

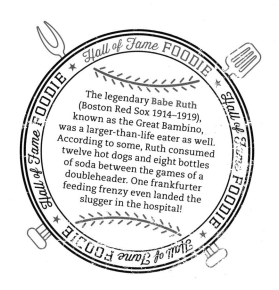

Hall of Fame FOODIE

The legendary Babe Ruth (Boston Red Sox 1914–1919), known as the Great Bambino, was a larger-than-life eater as well. According to some, Ruth consumed twelve hot dogs and eight bottles of soda between the games of a doubleheader. One frankfurter feeding frenzy even landed the slugger in the hospital!

MINI BOSTON CREAM PIES

PREP	COOK	MAKES
15	**2**	**4**
MINUTES	HOURS	PIES

	INGREDIENTS	
◇	1 3-ounce package	instant vanilla pudding mix
◇	2 cups	milk
◇	1	pound cake
◇	½ cup	semisweet chocolate chips
◇	¼ cup	heavy whipping cream
◇		
◇		

1. In a mixing bowl, combine the vanilla pudding mix and milk. Whisk until the mix is dissolved completely, about 2 minutes. Cover and store in a refrigerator for at least 2 hours.

2. Meanwhile, cut the cake lengthwise to make 1-inch thick sheets.

3. Using a juice glass, cut the cake into eight circles and set aside.

4. Fill the saucepan half full with water and place a heatproof mixing bowl on top, making sure the water does not touch the bottom of the bowl.

5. Place saucepan on the stove and heat the water to a simmer.

6. Add the chocolate and heavy cream to the bowl, stirring slowly until the chocolate melts and creates a smooth sauce. Turn off the burner.

7. To assemble the cakes, place one cake circle on the bottom, followed by pudding, then put a second cake circle on top to make a sandwich.

8. Pour about ¼ cup of the chocolate sauce on top of the cake. Repeat for the rest of the cakes. Allow to set for about 10 minutes before serving.

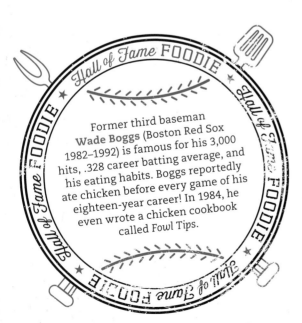

Hall of Fame FOODIE

Former third baseman **Wade Boggs** (Boston Red Sox 1982–1992) is famous for his 3,000 hits, .328 career batting average, and his eating habits. Boggs reportedly ate chicken before every game of his eighteen-year career! In 1984, he even wrote a chicken cookbook called *Fowl Tips*.

Condiment QUIZ

Forget ketchup and mustard! Today's stadium snacks come fully loaded with signature sauces. Can you name all the condiments in this collection? Remember, three strikes and you're out!

NYY

YANKEE STADIUM

LOCATION
Bronx, New York
OPENED
2009
CAPACITY
49,642
NICKNAMES
New Yankee Stadium
The House That Steinbrenner Built
The Bronx Bandbox

In 2009, the Yankees moved across the street, literally, from their old stadium to a new ballpark in the Bronx. The name moved with them as it's still called Yankee Stadium. Like the old stadium, the new ballpark has a classic, open feel — the playing field dimensions are even exactly same — only the new Yankee Stadium has some modern amenities like cup holders on all seats, party suites, and a towering, 101-foot wide HD scoreboard. The Bronx Bombers christened the new stadium with their 27th World Series title the year it opened. Oddly enough, they won their first World Series in 1923, when the old Yankee Stadium opened.

STEAK SANDWICH

with CREAMY PEPPERCORN SAUCE & GARLIC POTATO WEDGES

As one of the oldest teams in the league, the Yankees are experienced in providing quality ballpark food, starting with freshly made ribbon fries and famous New York hot dogs. Today, the stadium's food options range widely, from build-your-own-nachos stands to high-end steak joints. But this tender, sky-high steak sandwich will satisfy any Empire State appetite.

STEAK SANDWICH

PREP	COOK	MAKES
10	25	4
MINUTES	MINUTES	SANDWICHES

	INGREDIENTS	
◇	1	medium onion, sliced
◇	1	roasted red pepper
◇	2 tablespoons	olive oil, divided
◇	2 6-ounce	strip steaks
◇	4	ciabatta rolls
◇	dash	salt & pepper
◇	1 ounce	creamy peppercorn sauce
◇		

1 In a skillet, place 1 tablespoon olive oil and heat to medium. Add sliced onion and red pepper. Cook over medium heat until the onions soften and turn slightly brown, stirring occasionally.

2 Meanwhile, on a clean cutting board, season both sides of the steak with salt and pepper.

3 In another skillet, heat the remaining tablespoon of olive oil over medium-high heat.

4 Carefully place the steaks in the pan.

5 Cook for about 6–7 minutes, turn them over with tongs and cook another 6–7 minutes.

6 Remove the steaks, place on a plate, and loosely put foil over them. Allow to sit for 10 minutes.

7 While the steaks rest, prepare rolls by slicing in half crosswise, and make the peppercorn sauce. When the steaks are finished resting, slice thinly.

8 To assemble the sandwiches, spread 2 tablespoons of the peppercorn sauce on the bottom half of each ciabatta roll. Next, add about ¼ of the steak, followed by ¼ of the onion and pepper mix. Top with the second half of the roll. Serve immediately.

SAY WHAT?!

"YOU BETTER CUT THE PIZZA IN FOUR PIECES, BECAUSE I'M NOT HUNGRY ENOUGH TO EAT SIX."

YOGI BERRA
(CATCHER, NEW YORK YANKEES 1946-1963)

CREAMY PEPPERCORN SAUCE

PREP	COOK	MAKES
5	**0**	**4**
MINUTES	MINUTES	OUNCES

	INGREDIENTS	
◇	3 tablespoons	mayonnaise
◇	3 tablespoons	sour cream
◇	1 teaspoon	Dijon mustard
◇	½ teaspoon	Worcestershire sauce
◇	1 tablespoon	freshly ground pepper
◇	½ teaspoon	salt

GARLIC POTATO WEDGES

PREP	COOK	MAKES
10	**40**	**4**
MINUTES	MINUTES	SERVINGS

	INGREDIENTS	
◇	4	russet potatoes
◇	¼ cup	olive oil
◇	2 teaspoons	crushed garlic
◇	1 teaspoon	salt
◇	½ teaspoon	ground black pepper
◇	¼ cup	grated parmesan cheese
◇		

1. Combine all ingredients in a small mixing bowl and stir well.

2. Store any leftovers in an airtight container in the refrigerator for up to 3 days.

1. Preheat oven to 425°F and line baking sheet with parchment paper. Set aside. Peel and cut the potatoes into wedges.

2. In a mixing bowl, combine the potatoes, olive oil, crushed garlic, salt, and pepper. Stir until the potatoes are well coated.

3. Arrange the potatoes on the baking sheet, about ½ inch apart. Bake in the oven for about 15 minutes and then carefully flip them over using a spatula. Bake for an additional 15 minutes or until golden brown.

4. Sprinkle cheese over the potatoes and return to the oven for another 5–10 minutes or until the cheese is melted and slightly browned.

5. Remove from the oven and allow to cool slightly before serving.

TB

Tampa Bay Rays Baseball Club

TROPICANA FIELD

LOCATION
St. Petersburg, Florida
OPENED
1990
CAPACITY
31,042
NICKNAMES
The Trop
The Juicer

Tropicana Field was a case of "build it, and they will come." The park was completed in 1990, in St. Petersburg, just outside of Tampa, in hopes that a team would eventually call the stadium home. The expansion Tampa Bay Devil Rays joined the American League in 1998. The team's name was later shortened to just "Rays" in 2008. Tropicana Field is unique among modern-day ballparks. It is the only domed baseball stadium still in use, and it is one of just two parks with an artificial playing field. Another feature that sets it apart is its 10,000-gallon Rays Touch Tank, with actual stingrays — not players — just beyond the right-center-field wall.

CUBAN SANDWICH

with FRIED PLANTAINS

Just five hundred miles from Cuba, Tampa, Florida is bursting with Latin influence. In fact, the city was home to the first Cuban community in the United States. So it's no surprise that Tropicana Field is home to tropical drinks and festive foods, including the island's namesake dish: the Cuban. This tangy, meat-stuffed sandwich is always a home run!

CUBAN SANDWICH

PREP	COOK	MAKES
10	40	4
MINUTES	MINUTES	SANDWICHES

	INGREDIENTS	
◇	1 1-pound	pork tenderloin
◇	generous amount	salt & pepper
◇	2 tablespoons	olive oil
◇	4	ciabatta rolls
◇	4 teaspoons, divided	mustard
◇	12 slices, divided	smoked deli ham
◇	4 slices, divided	Swiss cheese
◇	4	dill pickle spears

YUCKY CHARMS

In 2008, Tropicana Field groundskeepers hung hot dogs inside a stadium locker — a good luck charm to their slumping team. Believe it or not, the Ray's started winning! When the rotting dogs mysteriously disappeared (and the team started losing), a picture of the hot dogs (and a couple of meatballs!) were hung up instead. That year, the Rays competed in the World Series, their most successful season to date.

1 First, prepare the pork. Preheat oven to 375°F. Place tenderloin on a cutting board and season generously with salt and pepper.

2 Place pork tenderloin on a baking sheet and drizzle olive oil over the top.

3 Bake in oven for 30–35 minutes or until no longer pink inside.

4 Remove from oven and cover with foil. Allow to rest for 10 minutes before slicing thinly.

5 To assemble sandwiches, slice each roll crosswise and spread 1 teaspoon of mustard on the bottom half of each.

6 Place 3 slices of ham on top of the mustard.

7 Add about ¼ of the pork slices on top of the ham, followed by a slice of Swiss cheese and a pickle spear.

8 Place the top of the bread on and serve immediately.

FRIED PLANTAINS

PREP	COOK	MAKES
5	**5**	**4**
MINUTES	MINUTES	SERVINGS

INGREDIENTS	
◇ 2 large	plantains, ripe
◇ 2 tablespoons	olive oil
◇ 1 teaspoon	salt

1 Peel the plantains and slice into ½-inch rounds.

2 Add oil to a skillet and heat on medium.

3 Carefully add the plantains (Be very careful! There might be splatters!) and cook for about 2 minutes, until golden brown. Flip them over and cook an additional minute.

4 Remove the plantains to a plate lined with paper towels. Sprinkle immediately with salt.

5 Allow to cool for 2 minutes before serving.

THE MUSTARD BULLPEN

While traditional Cuban sandwiches contain yellow mustard, don't be afraid to throw a changeup and sub in one of these mustard varieties:

Spicy Brown   Honey   Whole Grain   Dijon   Hot

TOR

Toronto Blue Jays Baseball Club

ROGERS CENTRE

LOCATION
Toronto, Ontario
OPENED
1989
CAPACITY
49,282
NICKNAMES
SkyDome
The Dome

The Blue Jays are the only Canadian team in the MLB. Their newest ballpark, the Rogers Centre, opened in 1989. It helped begin the era of retractable-roof stadiums, as it was the first ballpark to have one that functioned properly — unlike Olympic Stadium in Montreal, which was the first attempt at a retractable roof. Rogers Centre currently has an artificial playing surface, but team officials and fans alike are hoping a grass field will be installed in the near future. The CFL Argonauts also play at Rogers Centre — the pitcher's mound can be raised or lowered depending on if the home team is playing baseball or football. Also, the Renaissance Hotel is part of the stadium. Visitors can watch games from one of 70 rooms that overlook the playing field.

POUTINE

with APPLE BLONDIES WITH MAPLE GLAZE

Poutine, pronounced poo-TEEN, originated in Quebec, Canada, in the late 1950s. Since then, this hearty dish has become a favorite across the Great White North, including many concession stands at Rogers Centre. A concoction of thick, salty french fries, brown gravy, and cheese curds, this game-day snack is the ultimate triple play.

POUTINE

	PREP	COOK	MAKES
	15 MINUTES	**35** MINUTES	**4** SERVINGS

INGREDIENTS

◇	4	russet potatoes
◇	¼ cup	olive oil
◇	1 ½ teaspoons	salt, divided
◇	1 teaspoon	ground black pepper
◇	2 tablespoons	unsalted butter
◇	2 tablespoons	all-purpose flour
◇	1 ½ cups	beef broth
◇	1 teaspoon	Worcestershire sauce
◇	1 cup	cheddar cheese curds

POUTINE TIME LINE

1957 — Construction worker Eddy Lainesse orders a bag of fries at Café Idéal in Warwick, Quebec, Canada. He asks restaurant owner Fernand Lachance to mix in some cheese curds. The first "poutine" is born.

1964 — The Le Roy Jucep introduces poutine on its menu, complete with brown gravy. Restaurant owner Jean-Paul Roy officially named the concoction "poutine," a Québécois French pronunciation of the word "pudding."

1987 — First major fast food chain adds poutine to its menu.

2014 — "Poutine" is added to the Merriam-Webster dictionary.

2015 — Detroit Tigers unveil poutine hot dog at Comerica Park.

1 Preheat oven to 450°F and line a baking sheet with parchment paper. Set aside.

2 Peel and cut the potatoes into ¼-inch wide sticks, like french fries. Dry well with a paper towel and place in mixing bowl with olive oil, 1 teaspoon salt and ½ teaspoon ground black pepper. Stir until the potatoes are coated.

3 Arrange the potatoes on the baking sheet and place in the oven for 15 minutes, then flipping them with a spatula and baking an additional 15 minutes or until golden brown and crispy.

4 Meanwhile, make the sauce. In a saucepan over medium heat, melt the butter. Add the flour and whisk until the butter has absorbed the flour.

5 While whisking, pour in the broth and add the Worcestershire sauce. Continue to whisk until the sauce begins to bubble. Turn down the heat to a gentle simmer until the sauce thickens, about 5 minutes.

6 Season with ½ teaspoon salt and ½ teaspoon ground black pepper, adding more if necessary.

7 Serve on a large platter with edges, spread the french fries evenly. Sprinkle the cheese all over the fries, and then pour the sauce over the top. Serve immediately.

APPLE BLONDIES WITH MAPLE GLAZE

PREP	COOK	MAKES
15 MINUTES	**35** MINUTES	**12** BLONDIES

	INGREDIENTS	
◇	BLONDIES:	
◇	generous sprays	non-stick cooking spray
◇	½ cup (1 stick)	unsalted butter
◇	2	Granny Smith apples
◇	1 cup	flour
◇	2 teaspoons	ground cinnamon
◇	½ teaspoon	baking powder
◇	¼ teaspoon	baking soda
◇	¼ teaspoon	salt
◇	1	egg
◇	1 cup, packed	dark brown sugar
◇	1 teaspoon	vanilla extract
◇	¼ cup	chopped walnuts
◇		
◇	MAPLE GLAZE:	
◇	½ cup	powdered sugar
◇	¼ cup	pure maple syrup
◇	¼ teaspoon	vanilla extract
◇	2 tablespoons	water or milk
◇		

1 Slowly melt the butter over low heat in a saucepan. Set aside to cool.

2 Preheat oven to 350°F and generously spray a baking dish to prevent sticking.

3 Peel and core the apples, then chop into ½-inch cubes. Set aside.

4 In a large mixing bowl, combine flour, cinnamon, baking powder, baking soda, and salt. Stir to combine.

5 In a second mixing bowl, combine the cooled butter, egg, dark brown sugar, and vanilla extract. Whisk vigorously until the brown sugar is mostly dissolved.

6 Pour the liquids into the flour mixture and stir to combine. Add apples and walnuts, if using. Stir gently and pour into the baking dish.

7 Bake for 35 minutes or until a toothpick comes out clean after piercing the blondie. Allow to cool completely before glazing, about 1 hour.

8 While the blondies are baking, make the glaze. Combine the powdered sugar, maple syrup, vanilla extract, and water or milk in a small mixing bowl. Use a fork to mix until it forms a glaze. Add more water or milk if it is too thick, or more powdered sugar if it is too thin.

9 Finish the blondies by drizzling the glaze over the bars before cutting and serving.

U.S. CELLULAR FIELD

LOCATION	
Chicago, Illinois	
OPENED	
1991	
CAPACITY	
40,615	
NICKNAMES	
The Cell	
New Comiskey Park	

Opening in 1991 as "new" Comiskey Park — replacing the 81-year-old "old" Comiskey — the home of the White Sox was officially renamed U.S. Cellular Field in 2003. The Cell, as fans call it, towers above the South Side of Chicago, just off the city's busy Dan Ryan Expressway. Fans wandering the concourse can take in sculptures featuring White Sox legends, from Nellie Fox to Paul Konerko. Built just one year before a new wave of retro-style ballparks, many Chicago fans still long for their cozy, fan-friendly stadium of yesteryear. However, continued renovations have increased U.S. Cellular's appeal, and the giant, exploding scoreboard in center field — a holdover from old Comiskey — remains a fan favorite.

CHICAGO-STYLE HOT DOG

with CORN OFF THE COB

Those seeking the South Side's finest fare have a wealth of options. Dining staples include the city's famous deep-dish pizza and this Chicago-style hot dog, loaded with onions, relish, and a pickle spear. Fans also line up to chow down on the Cell's famous corn off the cob — sweet corn loaded with cheese and soaked in everything from butter to mayonnaise!

CHICAGO-STYLE HOT DOG

PREP	COOK	MAKES
10 MINUTES	5 MINUTES	4 DOGS

	INGREDIENTS	
◇	4	hot dogs
◇	3 cups	water
◇	4	hot dog buns
◇	1 tablespoon	butter, melted
◇	2 teaspoons	poppy seeds
◇	½	small onion
◇	1	medium tomato
◇	4 tablespoons	yellow mustard
◇	4 tablespoons	sweet pickle relish
◇	4	dill pickle spears
◇	4 tablespoons	jarred hot peppers
◇		

1 Add water to a skillet and bring to a simmer. Add hot dogs and cook for 5 minutes or until hot. Set aside.

2 Brush butter on outsides of the buns and sprinkle lightly with the poppy seeds. Set aside.

3 Chop the onion into small pieces, then chop the tomato into bite-sized chunks. Set aside.

4 Assemble the hot dogs by sprinkling ¼ of the onions inside the buns, followed by the hot dog. Then add ¼ of the tomatoes, followed by 1 tablespoon of mustard, 1 tablespoon of relish, a pickle spear, and 1 tablespoon of jarred hot peppers.

5 Serve immediately.

- -

HOLD THE Vegetables

Chicago Dogs are served on a poppy-seed bun and "dragged through the garden" with seven toppings: yellow mustard, green relish, onions, tomato, pickle spear, sport peppers, and celery salt. However, many food historians believe the original Chicago Dog was served on a plain, steamed bun with only three of these famous ingredients (mustard, onion, and sport peppers). It was also loaded with a heaping helping of hand-cut french fries! Today, this version of a Chicago Dog is known as a "Depression Dog" or a "Minimalist Dog." Use the french fries recipe on page 96 to create this historic hot dog!

- -

CORN OFF THE COB

	PREP	COOK	MAKES
	5 MINUTES	**10** MINUTES	**4** SERVINGS

	INGREDIENTS	
◇	4	frozen corn cobs
◇	½ cup	cheddar cheese
◇	2 tablespoons	butter
◇	to taste	salt and pepper
◇	to taste	paprika

1 Fill a large stockpot with water, then place on a burner at high heat. When the water comes to a boil, add the corn using tongs and reduce heat to medium to simmer. Cover and cook for about 10 minutes.

2 Meanwhile, get the topping ready. Shred the cheese with a box grater on the side with large holes. Melt the butter in a saucepan over low heat. Set both aside.

3 When the corn is done, carefully remove the cobs from the pot with tongs, and place on a cutting board.

4 Allow to cool for 5 minutes before standing each cob and sliding a chef's knife down the sides, allowing the corn kernels to fall onto the cutting board.

5 In a mixing bowl, combine the melted butter, cheese, and corn. Stir. Add salt and pepper to your liking, as well as paprika. Serve immediately.

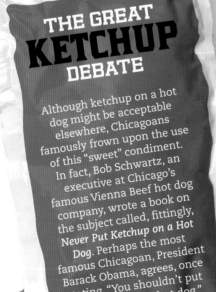

THE GREAT KETCHUP DEBATE

Although ketchup on a hot dog might be acceptable elsewhere, Chicagoans famously frown upon the use of this "sweet" condiment. In fact, Bob Schwartz, an executive at Chicago's famous Vienna Beef hot dog company, wrote a book on the subject called, fittingly, *Never Put Ketchup on a Hot Dog*. Perhaps the most famous Chicagoan, President Barack Obama, agrees, once stating, "You shouldn't put ketchup on your hot dog."

Chicagoans are not alone. According to the National Hot Dog and Sausage Council, based in Washington, DC, eaters should not use ketchup on their hot dogs after age 18! The Great Ketchup Debate continues. . .

PROGRESSIVE FIELD

LOCATION

Cleveland, Ohio

OPENED

1994

CAPACITY

38,000

NICKNAME

The Jake

The Indians opened their 1994 season playing in Jacobs Field. But The Jake's naming rights were later purchased, and the park is now called Progressive Field. Before the move to their new stadium, the team was considered one of the worst clubs in baseball. Shortly afterward, they made two trips to the World Series, only to lose both times, and were selling out games left and right. When the stadium's massive scoreboard was installed in 2004, it was the largest in all of sports. Recent renovations at Progressive Field have expanded the view of downtown Cleveland as well as added restaurants, social spaces, and other modern amenities.

PARMESAN-GARLIC POPCORN

with NUTTY CHOCOLATE DRIZZLE POPCORN & WATERMELON LEMONADE

Indians fans can go from downtown Cleveland to Progressive Field through the center-field entrance, which means there's a plethora of food choices in the area. But one of the stadium's signature foods is as classic as baseball itself: popcorn! This crunchy hand-snack is sold in several varieties throughout the park. Salty or sweet, popcorn is always a treat.

PARMESAN-GARLIC POPCORN

PREP	COOK	MAKES
5	5	6
MINUTES	MINUTES	SERVINGS

	INGREDIENTS	
◇	2 ounces	parmesan cheese
◇	3 tablespoons	butter
◇	1 cup	popping corn
◇	1 tablespoon	oil
◇	2 teaspoons	garlic salt
◇		

1. Shred the cheese using the small holes of a box grater, then melt the butter over low heat in a small saucepan. Set aside.

2. Add the oil and popping corn to the large pot and cover with lid. Set over medium heat until you start to hear the corn popping. Slide the pot back and forth over the heating element until you no longer hear the kernels popping. Remove from heat immediately.

3. Carefully pour the popped corn into a large mixing bowl and add the butter, cheese, and garlic salt. Mix well. Serve immediately.

WATERMELON LEMONADE

PREP	COOK	MAKES
10	0	2
MINUTES	MINUTES	QUARTS

	INGREDIENTS	
◇	4 cups	watermelon, chopped
◇	6 cups	lemonade
◇		

1. Place watermelon in a blender. Blend until pureed.

2. Place a sieve over the pitcher and pour watermelon puree through it. Discard the pulp left over.

3. Pour lemonade into the pitcher. Stir to combine. Pour in glasses with ice cubes.

NUTTY CHOCOLATE DRIZZLE POPCORN

PREP	COOK	MAKES
10 MINUTES	**5** MINUTES	**6** SERVINGS

	INGREDIENTS	
◇	1 cup	popping corn
◇	3 tablespoons	oil
◇	½ cup	semisweet chocolate chips
◇	½ cup	peanut butter chips
◇	¼ cup	butter
◇	½ cup	powdered sugar
◇		

1 Add the oil and popping corn to the large pot and cover with lid. Set over medium heat until you start to hear the corn popping. Slide the pot back and forth over the heating element until you no longer hear the kernels popping. Remove from heat immediately and set aside.

2 In a microwave-safe bowl, add the semisweet chocolate chips, peanut butter chips, and butter. Microwave at 50% for 30 seconds, then stir. Microwave an additional 30 seconds or until the chips and butter are melted and smooth.

3 Place the popped corn in a mixing bowl and drizzle the chocolate mixture over. Stir until all the popcorn is coated.

4 Sprinkle powdered sugar on top and mix until coated. Allow to rest for at least 30 minutes before serving.

POP ICON

Looking for an alternative to cooking popcorn with oil? Try an air popper, which pops corn kernels with hot air. In the mid-1970s, one of the first air poppers was invented in Cleveland, Ohio, making the city a true pop icon!

DET

Detroit Tigers Baseball Club

COMERICA PARK

LOCATION

Detroit, Michigan

OPENED

2000

CAPACITY

41,574

NICKNAMES

Comerica National Park

CoPa

Tigers don't roam just the outfield in downtown Detroit's Comerica Park. From the fifteen-foot tiger statue at the entrance to the two perched atop the left-field scoreboard — whose eyes light up after Detroit home runs and victories — the big cats are everywhere. Fans more interested in the baseball variety of Tigers enjoy Comerica Park's throwback-style field, complete with a strip of dirt between home plate and the pitcher's mound, as well as the Detroit skyline, visible over the left-field fence. Kids and adults alike delight in the park's fifty-foot Ferris wheel, complete with a dozen baseball-shaped cars that can seat up to five passengers each.

CONEY DOG

with ONION RINGS & APPLE CHERRY PUNCH

Comerica Park, built in 2000, caters to baseball fans who prefer more standard ballpark fare. Stadium favorites include street tacos, onion rings, and good old-fashioned corn dogs. But Coney Dogs fuel Detroit Tigers fans. Serve these meat-sauce-topped dogs with a side of thick onion rings and a sweet, refreshing punch for the ultimate Motor City meal.

CONEY DOG

PREP	COOK	MAKES
10 MINUTES	**30** MINUTES	**4** DOGS

	INGREDIENTS	
◇	1	bell pepper
◇	1	small onion
◇	½ pound	lean ground beef
◇		or turkey
◇	1 tablespoon	cumin
◇	1 tablespoon	chili powder
◇	1 teaspoon	paprika
◇	1 teaspoon	salt
◇	½ teaspoon	pepper
◇	1 15-ounce can	tomato sauce
◇	4	hot dogs
◇	4	hot dog buns
◇	4 tablespoons	yellow mustard
◇		

1. Cut the bell pepper and onion into small pieces. Set aside about 4 tablespoons of the onion for topping.

2. In a medium pot, combine the pepper, onion, and ground beef or turkey. Set heat to medium and cook until the meat is cooked, or no longer pink. Drain the fat.

3. Add the cumin, chili powder, paprika, salt, pepper, and tomato sauce.

4. Bring to a simmer and cook for about 20 minutes.

5. Meanwhile, heat the hot dogs in a skillet with 3 cups of water over medium heat.

6. To assemble the hot dogs, place a hot dog in a bun, followed by about ½ cup of the chili sauce, a sprinkling of onion, and a drizzle of mustard over the top. Serve immediately.

DETROIT CONEYS

Detroit Coneys, or Coney Islands, are made with heart — literally!
Beef hearts often flavor Motown's fine-ground meat sauce. Experiment
with the recipe above for your own signature Coney!

ONION RINGS

PREP	COOK	MAKES
10	20	4
MINUTES	MINUTES	SERVINGS

INGREDIENTS	
2	medium onions
1 cup	all-purpose flour
1 teaspoon	smoked paprika
1 ½ teaspoons	salt, divided
2	eggs
1 cup	bread crumbs
several spritzes	olive oil cooking spray

1 Preheat oven to 400°F. Line baking sheet with parchment paper and set aside.

2 Peel and slice the onions into ½-inch rings.

3 Place the flour on a plate and add paprika and half of the salt. Stir with a fork. Crack the eggs into a bowl and beat with a fork. Pour the bread crumbs on the second plate.

4 Dip each ring first in the flour, then egg, and then the bread crumbs.

5 Place rings flatly on the baking sheet and lightly spritz olive oil spray over the onions. Bake for 20 minutes. Remove from oven, salt, and cool slightly before serving.

APPLE-CHERRY PUNCH

PREP	COOK	MAKES
5	0	2
MINUTES	MINUTES	QUARTS

INGREDIENTS	
1 quart	apple juice
16 ounces	cherry juice
16 ounces	sparkling water
2 cups	ice cubes
4–6	maraschino cherries

1 Mix apple juice, cherry juice, and sparkling water in a pitcher.

2 Pour into glasses with ice cubes and a couple maraschino cherries.

KC

KAUFFMAN STADIUM

LOCATION
Kansas City, Missouri
OPENED
1973
CAPACITY
37,903
NICKNAMES
The K

Formerly known as Royals Stadium, Kauffman Stadium strikes the perfect blend between historic and modern amenities. It's the sixth-oldest big-league stadium still in use, yet its progressive architecture and an extensive 2009 remodel keep it feeling modern and new. The ballpark's trademark feature is its 322-foot waterfall display in center field, complete with fountains that spray water into the air before the game and between innings. Fans with a taste for baseball history can visit statues of Royals greats George Brett, Dick Howser, and Frank White in right field.

BARBECUE RIBS

with PICKLES & CORN BREAD MUFFINS

Kansas City proclaims itself the barbecue capital of America, and Kauffman Stadium doesn't fail to live up to that title. Fans can enjoy a rack of barbecued ribs, either on the concourse or in the countless rib joints sprinkled all around town. Pair that with some fresh-baked cornbread and home-style pickles for a true Kansas City dining experience.

BARBECUE RIBS

PREP	COOK	MAKES
10	**5**	**6**
MINUTES	HOURS	SERVINGS

	INGREDIENTS	
◇	2 racks	baby back ribs,
◇		silver skin removed
◇	1 cup	barbecue sauce, plus
◇		more for serving
◇	RIB RUB:	
◇	2/3 cup	brown sugar
◇	1/4 cup	smoked paprika
◇	2 tablespoons	black pepper
◇	1 tablespoon	kosher salt
◇	1 tablespoon	chili powder
◇	1 tablespoon	garlic powder
◇	1 tablespoon	onion powder
◇	1 tablespoon	dry mustard

1 Preheat oven to 250°F. Combine the rib rub ingredients in a small mixing bowl and stir.

2 Place rib racks on the cutting board. Sprinkle the rib rub all over the racks, top and bottom.

3 Make foil packets by tearing two sheets of aluminum foil per rack that are slightly longer than the rib racks. Place the ribs on top of the first foil sheet. Then place the second foil sheet over the ribs and seal tightly. Repeat for the second rack of ribs.

4 Put the foil packets on a baking sheet and place in the oven. Bake for about 4–5 hours.

5 Heat grill to 450°F. Carefully remove the foil and use tongs to place the ribs on the grill.

6 Brush the ribs with barbecue sauce on all sides and allow to cook for about 5 minutes on each side.

7 Remove the ribs from the grill and serve immediately with additional sauce on the side.

BARBECUE REGIONS

Several U.S. regions are known for their distinct BBQ styles. Some prefer "wet" barbecue (with sauce) while others prefer "dry" BBQ (without sauce).

KANSAS CITY STYLE
STYLE: Tangy and sweet
MEAT: Burnt ends
SAUCE: Tomato- and molasses-based

TEXAS STYLE
STYLE: Bold and spicy
MEAT: Beef brisket
SAUCE: Thin, spicy, tomato-based

PICKLES

	PREP	COOK	MAKES
	5 MINUTES	**1** DAY	**1** QUART

INGREDIENTS

◇	1	large English cucumber
◇	1	small onion
◇	1 cup	white vinegar
◇	1 cup	granulated sugar
◇	1 teaspoon	mustard seed
◇	1 teaspoon	celery seed
◇	1 teaspoon	dill seed
◇	1 teaspoon	black peppercorns
◇	1 teaspoon	salt
◇	½ teaspoon	turmeric

1 Slice the cucumber into ¼-inch rounds. Place in a quart-sized jar or plastic container and set aside.

2 Slice the onion into ¼-inch rounds and add to the cucumbers. Put the lid on and shake to mix up the cucumbers and onion. Remove lid and set aside.

3 In a saucepan, add the vinegar, sugar, mustard seed, celery seed, dill seed, black peppercorns, salt, and turmeric. Heat over medium-high heat until it reaches a boil. Whisk to dissolve the sugar.

4 Pour the hot liquid into the jar over the cucumber/onion mix. Allow to cool for about 30 minutes before placing the lid on and moving to the refrigerator.

5 Allow to sit for at least 1 day before eating. Store leftovers in the refrigerator for up to 1 week.

MEMPHIS STYLE
STYLE: Dry rub
MEAT: Pork ribs
RUB: Salt, pepper, paprika, cayenne, and sugar

SOUTH CAROLINA STYLE
STYLE: German-influenced
MEAT: A whole pig
SAUCE: Mustard-based

CORNBREAD MUFFINS

PREP	COOK	MAKES
5	**25**	**12**
MINUTES	MINUTES	MUFFINS

INGREDIENTS

◇	3 tablespoons	pickled jalapeños
◇	1 cup	sharp cheddar cheese
◇	1 ¼ cup	finely ground cornmeal
◇	1 cup	all–purpose flour
◇	2 ½ teaspoons	baking powder
◇	½ teaspoon	salt
◇	⅓ cup	honey
◇	1 cup	buttermilk
◇	2	large eggs
◇	¼ cup	butter
◇	8 ounces	frozen corn

1 Preheat oven to 375°F. Chop the jalapeños very finely and set aside.

2 Grate the cheddar cheese and set aside.

3 Combine the cornmeal, flour, baking powder, and salt in a mixing bowl.

4 Melt the butter in a small saucepan and set aside for the following step.

5 In a second mixing bowl, whisk together the honey, buttermilk, eggs, and melted butter.

6 Pour the liquid ingredients into the dry ingredients and stir until just combined.

7 Stir in the cheese, corn, and jalapeños.

8 Place muffin liners into a muffin pan and scoop batter into the liners. Fill two-thirds full.

9 Bake for 20–22 minutes or until a toothpick inserted comes out clean.

10 Serve warm or at room temperature.

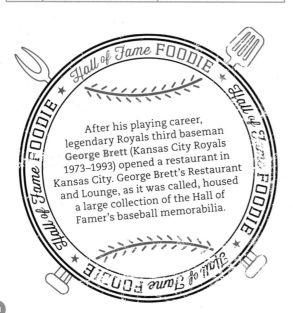

Hall of Fame FOODIE

After his playing career, legendary Royals third baseman **George Brett** (Kansas City Royals 1973–1993) opened a restaurant in Kansas City. George Brett's Restaurant and Lounge, as it was called, housed a large collection of the Hall of Famer's baseball memorabilia.

BALLPARK ★ FOODS
HALL OF FAME

★ Even after long concession-stand careers, these veteran eats are far from retirement. ★

HOT DOG

★ BALLPARK FOODS HALL OF FAME INDUCTEE ★

SOFT PRETZEL

★ BALLPARK FOODS HALL OF FAME INDUCTEE ★

PEANUTS

★ BALLPARK FOODS HALL OF FAME INDUCTEE ★

POPCORN

★ BALLPARK FOODS HALL OF FAME INDUCTEE ★

ICE CREAM

★ BALLPARK FOODS HALL OF FAME INDUCTEE ★

CARAMEL CORN
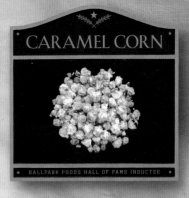
★ BALLPARK FOODS HALL OF FAME INDUCTEE ★

SUNFLOWER SEEDS

★ BALLPARK FOODS HALL OF FAME INDUCTEE ★

NACHOS
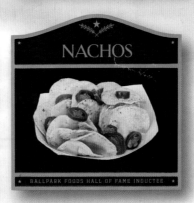
★ BALLPARK FOODS HALL OF FAME INDUCTEE ★

COTTON CANDY

★ BALLPARK FOODS HALL OF FAME INDUCTEE ★

MIN

Minnesota Twins Baseball Club

TARGET FIELD

LOCATION	
Minneapolis, Minnesota	
OPENED	
2010	
CAPACITY	
39,021	

After decades of playing inside the cavernous Metrodome, the Minnesota Twins stepped back out under the sky with the opening of Target Field in 2010. The new ballpark provides spectacular views of downtown Minneapolis along with being a great venue for baseball. The stadium's relatively small footprint gives it a cozy, intimate feeling, while its downtown location has revitalized the city. The park's most distinct feature, a giant mechanical sign of the Twins's original team logo, illuminates in center field during home run celebrations.

CHEDDAR-BACON STUFFED BURGER
with APPLE PIE-ON-A-STICK

Fans needn't go home hungry at Target Field! Food options throughout the stadium feature local faves, including walleye, wild rice soup, and just about anything on a stick — a Minnesota State Fair tradition. Those looking for the Twin Cities' most famous dish can head to the upper concourse for a "Jucy Lucy," a hamburger stuffed with molten cheese.

CHEDDAR-BACON STUFFED BURGER

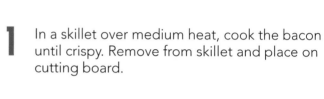

PREP	COOK	MAKES
10 MINUTES	20 MINUTES	4 BURGERS

INGREDIENTS

◇	4	strips bacon
◇	1 ½ pounds	ground beef or
◇		turkey
◇	4	slices cheddar cheese
◇	dash	salt & pepper
◇	4	hamburger buns
◇	optional fixings: ketchup, mustard, lettuce,	
◇	pickles, and/or tomatoes	

1 In a skillet over medium heat, cook the bacon until crispy. Remove from skillet and place on cutting board.

2 Chop the cooked bacon into small pieces and set aside.

3 Separate the meat into 8 equal pieces and form round patties.

4 Place a piece of bacon and a slice of cheese onto 4 of the burgers.

5 Over each burger with cheese and bacon, press a remaining patty on top of each one, sealing the sides well.

6 Season each side with salt and pepper and heat a second skillet over medium heat. When the pan is hot, place the burgers in the pan. Cook for about 10 minutes per side, or until no longer pink inside.

7 Serve on hamburger buns with your favorite toppings.

BREAKFAST OF CHAMPIONS

After their 1987 World Series victory, the Minnesota Twins became the first team to be featured on a box of Wheaties, a cereal made by the Minnesota-based company General Mills.

APPLE PIE-ON-A-STICK

PREP	COOK	MAKES
15 MINUTES	20 MINUTES	8 STICKS

INGREDIENTS

◇	2	refrigerated pie crusts
◇	1 can	apple pie filling
◇	1	egg
◇	2 tablespoons	cool water

1 Preheat oven and line baking sheet with parchment paper. Set aside.

2 Roll out the pie crusts and cut out 16 small circles using a juice glass.

3 Place craft sticks on 8 of the dough circles with the top of the stick in the center of the dough.

4 Dollop 1 heaping teaspoon of pie filling in the center of the dough circles with a stick.

5 In a mixing bowl, whisk the egg and water together.

6 Using a pastry brush, paint some of the egg wash around the edges of the dough circles with apple pie filling.

7 Set the other 8 dough circles over the pie filling and press to seal. Crimp the edges by pressing a fork around the circle.

8 Brush remaining egg wash over the top of the pie, and then cut a small X in the center of each pie.

9 Carefully transfer to the baking sheets and bake for about 20 minutes or until golden brown.

10 Allow to cool for 10 minutes before serving.

- -

HALL OF FAME *Foodies*

Several concession stands and restaurants at Target Field feature the nicknames of Minnesota Twins legends.

FRANKIE V's ITALIAN — Frank Viola, Minnesota Twins, 1982–1989

SEÑOR SMOKE'S — Juan Berenguer, Minnesota Twins, 1987–1990

HRBEK'S RESTAURANT — Kent Hrbek, Minnesota Twins, 1981–1994

TONY O's CUBAN SANDWICHES — Tony Oliva, Minnesota Twins, 1962–1976

HOU

Houston Astros Baseball Club

MINUTE MAID PARK

LOCATION	
Houston, Texas	
OPENED	
2000	
CAPACITY	
41,574	
NICKNAMES	
The Juice Box	

The Astros' old home, the Astrodome, built in 1965, began the trend of domed stadiums with artificial playing surfaces. It even inspired the name Astroturf for fake grass. However, in 2000, Houston constructed Minute Maid Park, which has a grass field, and a retractable roof, that protect players and fans from the heat of the Texas summer sun. One of the park's most unique features, that is not seen at any other park, is located in center field. Between the wall and warning track is Tal's Hill, a small, 90-foot wide embankment of grass that is part of the playing field.

PIZZA STUFFED BAKED POTATO

with ICED SWEET LEMON TEA

Tex-Mex is the blending of American and Mexican dishes, and it's a dominant food choice throughout Minute Maid Park. Fans can get cooked-to-order fajitas, fried tacos, and chipotle chicken nachos. But Texas-sized stuffed baked potatoes remain an Astros fan favorite. Fully loaded with a variety of ooey-gooey toppings, this meal is a grand slam!

PIZZA STUFFED BAKED POTATO

PREP	COOK	MAKES
5	**1¼**	**4**
MINUTES	HOURS	POTATOES

INGREDIENTS

◇	olive oil	for coating potatoes
◇	2	large baking potatoes
◇	½ cup	marinara sauce
◇		(see page 115)
◇	4 ounces	mozzarella cheese
◇	optional toppings: mini pepperonis, ham, onion,	
◇	peppers, mushrooms	

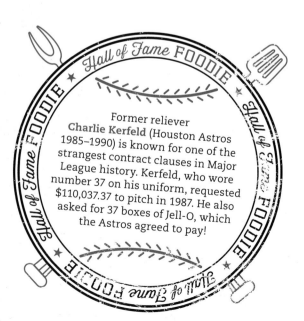

Former reliever **Charlie Kerfeld** (Houston Astros 1985–1990) is known for one of the strangest contract clauses in Major League history. Kerfeld, who wore number 37 on his uniform, requested $110,037.37 to pitch in 1987. He also asked for 37 boxes of Jell-O, which the Astros agreed to pay!

1 Preheat oven to 375°F. Wash and dry potatoes well. Poke holes by piercing a fork through the skin on each potato 3 or 4 times.

2 Lightly coat the potatoes with olive oil and place on oven rack. Bake for 1 hour or until tender.

3 Meanwhile, get your toppings ready. Grate the cheese, slice onions, peppers, mushrooms, and/or ham. Set aside.

4 When the potatoes are done, remove from the oven. While holding potatoes with an oven mitt or kitchen towel, carefully slice them in half lengthwise.

5 Place the potato halves on a baking sheet and lightly mash with a fork.

6 Spoon about 2 tablespoons of marinara sauce, followed by ¼ of the cheese, and then your favorite toppings on each potato.

7 Place back in the oven until the cheese is melted and slightly browned and serve immediately.

ICED SWEET LEMON TEA

PREP	COOK	MAKES
5	**0**	**2**
MINUTES	MINUTES	QUARTS

	INGREDIENTS	
◇	1 quart	lemonade
◇	1 quart	iced tea
◇	ice cubes and lemon slices, for serving	
◇		

1 Mix lemonade and iced tea in a pitcher.

2 Serve in glasses with ice cubes and a lemon slice for garnish.

GO BIG OR GO HOME

Everything is bigger in Texas — especially the food! And megasized meals have dug in at a number of ballparks. Here are a few reasons why professional baseball is known as the BIG leagues!

THE CHOOMONGUS

WHAT IS IT?
A two-foot long Korean beef sandwich, topped with spicy slaw and sriracha mayo

WHERE TO GET IT?
Texas Rangers's Globe Life Park

HOW MUCH?
$26

THE D-BAT DOG

WHAT IS IT?
An 18-inch corn dog, loaded with jalapeños, bacon, and cheese

WHERE TO GET IT?
Arizona Diamondbacks's Chase Field

HOW MUCH?
$25

THE BANANA SPLIT SUNDAE HELMET

WHAT IS IT?
Twelve scoops of vanilla, chocolate, and strawberry ice cream, topped with syrup, two bananas, whipped cream, and cherries

WHERE TO GET IT?
Chicago White Sox's U.S. Cellular Field

HOW MUCH?
$17

THE FAN VS. FOOD BURGER

WHAT IS IT?
A four-pound cheeseburger with all the fixings, including bacon, served with one pound of french fries

WHERE TO GET IT?
Tampa Bay Rays's Tropicana Field

HOW MUCH?
$30

THE WALK OFF

WHAT IS IT?
A sausage wrapped in pretzel roll and topped with in melted crab dip

WHERE TO GET IT?
Oriole Park at Camden Yards

HOW MUCH?
$15

LAA

ANGEL STADIUM
OF ANAHEIM

LOCATION
Anaheim, California
OPENED
1966
CAPACITY
45,957
NICKNAMES
The Big A

Opening for the 1966 season, Angel Stadium of Anaheim is one of the oldest stadiums in baseball. Yet, it doesn't look its age as it has a retro design that is so popular today. The stadium even has bleacher seats in the outfield. Known as the Big A, the stadium also features the "California spectacular" in left center field. This mountain landscape has trees, a stream, and erupting geysers. In the ballpark's long history, visitors have witnessed some great moments, from Reggie Jackson's 500th home run to George Brett's 3,000th hit, and a World Series title in 2002.

LOS ANGELES-STYLE HOT DOG

with RANCH SWEET POTATO FRIES & ORANGE DREAM PUNCH

The classic hot dog can be a heavenly and filling treat at the Angel Stadium of Anaheim. The Legends Dog is a foot-long frank covered with barbecued brisket, and the Big A's signature Halo Dog is wrapped in bacon and topped with charro beans, peppers, pico de gallo, and shredded cheese. The only real decision is which dog to lead off with!

LOS ANGELES-STYLE HOT DOG

PREP	COOK	MAKES
15	**5**	**4**
MINUTES	MINUTES	DOGS

	INGREDIENTS	
◇	HOT DOGS:	
◇	4	slices bacon
◇	1	small onion
◇	1 teaspoon	olive oil
◇	1 8-ounce can	pinto beans in
◇		chili sauce
◇	4	hot dogs
◇	4	hot dog buns
◇	1 cup	pico de gallo
◇	½ cup	grated cheddar cheese
◇		
◇	PICO DE GALLO:	
◇	1	medium tomato
◇	1	small onion
◇	1	small jalapeño
◇	½ teaspoon	salt
◇	½ teaspoon	pepper
◇		
◇		
◇		

1 Place the bacon in a skillet over medium heat. Fry until crispy. Remove to a paper-towel-lined plate to cool.

2 Peel the onion and slice into thin pieces. Add olive oil to a second skillet and heat over a medium burner. Add onion and sauté until slightly browned. Set aside.

3 Add beans to a saucepan and heat over medium until hot. Set aside.

4 Place the hot dogs in 3 cups of water in a third skillet. Bring to a simmer and cook for 5 minutes.

5 Chop the tomato and onion into small pieces and place in mixing bowl.

6 Cut the jalapeño in half lengthwise and scoop out the white inner part and seeds.

7 Chop the jalapeño into small pieces and add to the mixing bowl along with the salt and pepper.

8 Stir to combine. Store leftover pico de gallo in an airtight container in refrigerator for up to one week.

9 To assemble the hot dog, place a hot dog in a bun, slide a slice of bacon alongside the hot dog and put ¼ of the beans on top, followed by ¼ of the onions, 2 tablespoons of pico de gallo, and finally sprinkle with ¼ of the grated cheese. Repeat for the remaining hot dogs.

RANCH SWEET POTATO FRIES

PREP	COOK	MAKES
10	30	4
MINUTES	MINUTES	SERVINGS

INGREDIENTS	
◇ 2	medium sweet potatoes
◇ 1 tablespoon	olive oil
◇ 1 teaspoon	garlic powder
◇ 1 teaspoon	onion powder
◇ ½ teaspoon	dill
◇ 1 teaspoon	paprika
◇ 1 teaspoon	ground black pepper
◇ 1 teaspoon	salt
◇ 1 tablespoon	dried parsley

1. Preheat oven to 400°F and line a baking sheet with parchment paper. Set aside.

2. Peel and cut the potatoes into ½-inch-wide sticks. Place in a mixing bowl.

3. Add the olive oil, garlic powder, onion powder, dill, paprika, ground black pepper, salt, and dried parsley to the mixing bowl. Stir to combine and pour on the baking sheet.

4. Separate the potatoes so they lay flat on the baking sheet.

5. Bake for 15 minutes, then flip them over using a spatula and bake an additional 15 minutes or until slightly browned and crispy. Serve hot.

ORANGE DREAM PUNCH

PREP	COOK	MAKES
5	0	2
MINUTES	MINUTES	QUARTS

INGREDIENTS	
◇ 1 quart	orange juice
◇ 1 quart	cream soda
◇ 2 small scoops	orange sherbet

1. Combine the orange juice and cream soda in a pitcher. Stir well.

2. To serve, scoop a small amount of sherbet in a glass, then pour the punch to fill it.

OAK

Oakland Athletics Baseball Club

O.CO COLISEUM

LOCATION
Oakland, California
OPENED
1966
CAPACITY
35,067
NICKNAMES
Oakland Coliseum

O.co Coliseum opened in 1966, but it was the NFL's Raiders that first called it home. The A's didn't play there until 1968, when they moved from Kansas City to Oakland. In an era when MLB teams are building baseball-only parks, a multipurpose stadium like O.co Coliseum is a rarity. It's also one of the smallest ballparks, both in the MLB and NFL. Yet it has seen four World Series titles and has been home to greats like Rickey Henderson, who holds the all-time record for stolen bases, and Reggie Jackson.

SHRIMP QUESADILLAS

with GUACAMOLE & STRAWBERRY-MANGO PUNCH

Located on San Francisco Bay, Oakland's proximity to the Pacific Ocean heavily influences the local cuisine. Like other California ballparks, the Mexican impact on food culture is also significant. A combination of these two influences makes up some of O.co Coliseum's best diamond dishes, from Baja tacos to these flaky, cheese—smothered shrimp quesadillas.

SHRIMP QUESADILLAS

PREP	COOK	MAKES
10	**10**	**4**
MINUTES	MINUTES	QUESADILLAS

INGREDIENTS

◇	1 pound	tail-off shrimp,
◇		peeled and deveined
◇	1 tablespoon + 1 teaspoon	olive oil, divided
◇	1 teaspoon	salt
◇	½ teaspoon	ground black pepper
◇	½ jar	roasted red peppers
◇	1	small onion
◇	8 ounces	Monterey Jack cheese
◇	4	large flour tortillas
◇	2 tablespoons	butter, divided
◇	2 ounces	sour cream
◇	2 ounces	salsa
◇	4 ounces	guacamole

1. In a skillet over medium heat, add 1 tablespoon olive oil. When oil is hot, add shrimp. Sprinkle with salt and pepper while it cooks.

2. Cook shrimp about 2 minutes per side or until pink. Remove from heat and set aside.

3. Chop the onion and slice the roasted red peppers. Add to a second skillet with 1 teaspoon olive oil and sauté over medium heat until tender, about 4 minutes.

4. While the onions and peppers cook, grate the cheese. Set aside.

5. To assemble quesadillas, in a third skillet, add one tablespoon butter over medium-low heat.

6. Quickly add the first tortilla, followed by ¼ of the cheese, ½ of the onion/pepper mixture, ½ of the shrimp, ¼ of the cheese, then top with a tortilla. Cook until the first tortilla is lightly browned on the bottom, about 2–3 minutes.

7. Using a spatula, carefully flip the quesadilla over to cook the other side for another 2–3 minutes.

8. Remove from heat to a cutting board and cool for 3 minutes before cutting into wedges.

9. Repeat for the other quesadillas. Serve with sour cream, salsa, and guacamole.

GUACAMOLE

PREP	COOK	MAKES
15	**0**	**4**
MINUTES	MINUTES	OUNCES

INGREDIENTS

◇	2	ripe avocados
◇	¼ bunch	cilantro, chopped
◇	1	lime
◇	½ teaspoon	salt
◇	½ teaspoon	black pepper
◇	1 clove	garlic, chopped finely
◇		

1 Have an adult cut the avocados in half and remove the pits.

2 Use a spoon to scoop out the avocado pulp from the skin and place it in a large mixing bowl.

3 Slice the lime in half and squeeze the juice into the mixing bowl.

4 Add the remaining ingredients. Lightly mash the avocado until it is well blended with the other ingredients. Cover and refrigerate for 1 hour before serving.

STRAWBERRY-MANGO PUNCH

PREP	COOK	MAKES
10	**0**	**2**
MINUTES	MINUTES	QUARTS

INGREDIENTS

◇	1 cup	frozen mango
◇	1 cup	frozen strawberries
◇	2 cups	orange-peach-mango juice
◇	1 quart	lemon-lime soda
◇	ice cubes and strawberries, for garnish	
◇		

 In a blender, combine mango, strawberries, and juice. Blend until smooth.

 Pour blended mixture in a pitcher along with the lemon-lime soda.

3 Serve in glasses with ice cubes and a strawberry for garnish.

SEA

Seattle Mariners Baseball Club

SAFECO FIELD

LOCATION	
Seattle, Washington	
OPENED	
1999	
CAPACITY	
47,574	
NICKNAMES	
The Safe	

Located in downtown Seattle, Safeco Field offers fans the best of both worlds. A retractable roof allows fans to see the Seattle skyline and Puget Sound sunsets on clear evenings, while keeping the field dry during the Pacific Northwest's frequent rain showers. "The Safe" is a classic baseball park, with real grass and flawless sight lines. The park's famous chandelier, constructed of 1,000 resin baseball bats, hangs over the home plate entrance, while "the Mitt" is a 9-foot bronze baseball glove and popular photo opportunity.

SANDWICH SUSHI

with SWEET SUSHI

Safeco mirrors Seattle in its wide range of food choices, from fresh sushi to barbecue to spicy pad thai. Fans in the mood for something a bit heavier can enjoy the stadium's garlic fries and bacon-wrapped hot dogs. After the game, fans have a wealth of choices in nearby restaurants, from Korean steakhouses to oyster joints to traditional sports grills

SANDWICH SUSHI

PREP	COOK	MAKES
10 MINUTES	**2** HOURS	**4** ROLLS

		INGREDIENTS
◇	4 ounces	cheddar cheese
◇	8 ounces	cream cheese, softened
◇		to room temperature
◇	4	large spinach tortillas
◇	8	slices deli meat such as
◇		ham, turkey, roast
◇		beef, or salami
◇	8	dill pickles

1 Grate the cheddar cheese and set aside.

2 Using a spatula, evenly spread 2 ounces of cream cheese on each tortilla, all the way to the edges.

3 Sprinkle ¼ of the cheddar cheese over the cream cheese.

4 Place 2 slices of deli meat on top to cover the cheese.

5 Place 2 dill pickles next, near the edge closest to you.

6 Roll tightly, starting from the bottom. Repeat with the remaining tortillas.

7 Wrap with plastic wrap and place in refrigerator for 2 hours.

8 To serve, unwrap the roll-ups and slice into 2-inch rounds.

9 Store leftovers in an airtight container in refrigerator for up to 3 days.

THE ICHIROLL

At Safeco Field, sushi is a popular — and somewhat unexpected — success, much like Ichiro Suzuki (Seattle Mariners 2001–2012). So it's no surprise the former Mariner right fielder got a spicy tuna roll named after him: the Ichiroll. During his time with the Mariners, Suzuki broke the single-season record for hits with 262, while his roll became a hit with fans!

SWEET SUSHI

	PREP	COOK	MAKES
	30 MINUTES	**0** HOURS	**16** PIECES

	INGREDIENTS	
◇	2 tablespoons	butter
◇	15	standard marshmallows
◇	3 cups	crispy rice cereal
◇	1 cup	fruit leathers
◇	1 cup	fish gummies

1 In a large saucepan, add the butter and marshmallows. Place over medium heat until melted, stirring frequently. Add the rice cereal and stir until well coated. Set aside to cool slightly.

2 Carefully scoop out small amounts with a tablespoon and shape into 8 ovals and 8 cylinders. Set aside to cool completely. A tip: Spray your hands with cooking spray to prevent sticky fingers!

3 In the meantime, slice the fruit leathers into strips the width of the cylinders.

4 For the ovals, cut thin strips of the fruit leather, about ½-inch thick.

5 To assemble, wrap the strips around the cylinders and for the ovals, place a fish on top and then wrap a thin strip around, pressing together at the bottom of the rice treat.

6 Serve immediately. Store leftovers in an airtight container at room temperature for up to 3 days.

Hall of Fame FOODIE

Baseball players chew plenty of gum, but **Felix Hernandez** (Seattle Mariners 2005–present) is a big-league chewer! The All-Star pitcher starts each game with three sticks of gum, and then refreshes with three new sticks between every inning.

TEX

Texas Rangers Baseball Club

GLOBE LIFE PARK
IN ARLINGTON

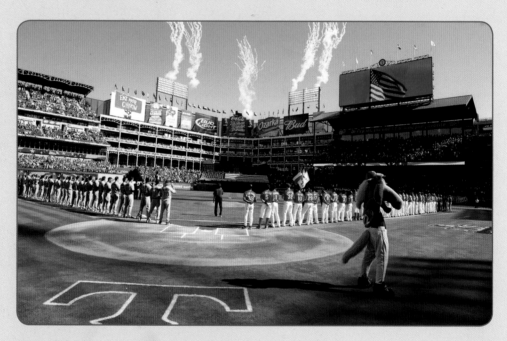

LOCATION
Arlington, Texas
OPENED
1994
CAPACITY
48,114
NICKNAMES
The Ballpark in Arlington
The Temple
The Globe

Completed in 1994, the Rangers' ballpark has gone through several name changes before settling on Globe Life Park. The park was built at a time when many other stadiums were drawing on past ballparks for inspiration, thus Globe Life Park's red-brick facade and arches. There is even a brick Walk of Fame inside the park that displays information of past Rangers. And some legends of the game, from strikeout king Nolan Ryan to phenom catcher Ivan Rodriquez have donned Rangers uniforms.

STEAK FAJITAS

with PECAN PIE BITES

The state of Texas is known for doing things big, and that carries over to its ballpark food. The stadium doesn't just offer foot-long dogs as the Choomongous is a two-foot-long beef teriyaki sandwich topped with spicy slaw. And then there's bacon — from bacon cotton candy to bacon-wrapped hot dogs and bacon on a stick.

STEAK FAJITAS

PREP	COOK	MAKES
10 MINUTES	**15** MINUTES	**4** FAJITAS

	INGREDIENTS	
◇	2 6-ounce	strip steaks
◇	1	bell pepper
◇	1	medium onion
◇	1 tablespoon	olive oil
◇	1 teaspoon	salt
◇	½ teaspoon	ground black pepper
◇	1 teaspoon	cumin
◇	1 teaspoon	chili powder
◇	¼ teaspoon	cayenne pepper
◇	8	flour tortillas
◇ ◇	optional toppings: grated cheese, sour cream, and guacamole (see page 65)	

1 Slice the steaks thinly and set aside.

2 Cut the top off the pepper, and then slice in half lengthwise. Scoop out the seeds and white parts. Slice into ¼-inch strips and set aside.

3 Peel and slice the onion into ¼-inch strips and set aside.

4 In a skillet, heat the oil over medium-high heat. When the oil is hot, add the steak. Cook for about 5 minutes, stirring every minute or two. After the meat has browned, reduce the heat to medium and then add the peppers, onions, salt, pepper, cumin, chili powder, and cayenne pepper.

5 Sauté for an additional 10 minutes or until the vegetables have begun to soften.

6 To assemble, place some meat/onion/pepper mixture into flour tortillas along with desired toppings and serve immediately.

TOP DOG

Where can you find the Major League's largest hot dog? Texas, of course! At Globe Life Park, hungry fans can take a crack at the "Boomstick," a two-foot-long hot dog covered in chili, cheese, and onions. The record-breaking (and gut-busting) dog is named after former Ranger right fielder Nelson Cruz's moniker (Texas Rangers, 2006–2013).

PECAN PIE BITES

	PREP	COOK	MAKES
	10 MINUTES	**2** HOURS	**16** BITES

	INGREDIENTS	
◇	12	pecan shortbread cookies
◇	4 ounces	cream cheese,
◇		softened to
◇		room temperature
◇	1/4 teaspoon	vanilla extract
◇	3/4 pound	vanilla almond bark
◇	1/4 cup	pecan chips

Hall of Fame FOODIE

The night before every start, pitcher **Derek Holland** (Texas Rangers 2009–present) orders exactly $30 worth of grub at his favorite fast food restaurant!

1 In a zip-top bag, put the cookies in and seal closed. Smash with a rolling pin until crushed into small crumbs.

2 Add the crumbs to a mixing bowl along with the cream cheese and vanilla extract. Stir until combined and then scoop out even tablespoons and roll between hands to make balls.

3 Set on a cookie sheet and refrigerate for 1 hour to set.

4 Meanwhile, melt the vanilla almond bark in a saucepan over low heat, stirring occasionally, and line a baking sheet with parchment paper and set aside.

5 When the bites are finished setting, drop one in the almond bark and remove with two forks, allowing the excess to drip off.

6 Carefully place on the lined baking sheet and sprinkle it with a pinch of pecan chips. Repeat for the rest of the bites.

7 Place dipped bites in refrigerator for an additional hour to set the coating before serving. Store in airtight container in refrigerator for up to 3 days.

National League

TURNER FIELD

LOCATION
Atlanta, Georgia
OPENED
1997
CAPACITY
49,586
NICKNAMES
The Ted

The Braves have been calling Turner Field home since 1997. Named after media mogul and team owner, Ted Turner, this stadium has helped guide the design of future ballparks. It's both baseball and fan friendly as visitors can walk around the lower concourse and still keep an eye on the game while getting something to nosh on. But the Braves' stay at the Ted, as locals call it, is about to end. Their lease is up in 2016, and a new stadium is already in the works. In 2017, the team will be playing at Sun Trust Park in Cobb County, just north of Atlanta, Georgia.

SHRIMP PO' BOY

with SWEET 'N' SPICY COLESLAW & PEACH SMOOTHIE

While at the Ted, one fan fave is the Yicketty Yamwich — inspired by Chipper Jones's slang term for a home run. This sandwich is like a grilled cheese stuffed with braised short ribs and spinach, and features a spiced apple butter. But there are many southern treats to feast on from pulled pork sandwiches to this flavorful, slaw-stuffed shrimp po' boy.

SHRIMP PO' BOY

PREP	COOK	MAKES
10	6	4
MINUTES	MINUTES	SANDWICHES

INGREDIENTS

◇	2 tablespoons	all-purpose flour
◇	1 teaspoon	seafood seasoning
◇	1 teaspoon	paprika
◇	½ teaspoon	salt
◇	½ teaspoon	ground black pepper
◇	½ pound	peeled, deveined,
◇		tail-off shrimp
◇	1 tablespoon	olive oil
◇	4	French sandwich rolls,
◇		split in half
◇	4 ounces	Sweet 'n' Spicy Coleslaw
◇	10–12	pickle slices

1 Mix the flour, seafood seasoning, paprika, salt, and black pepper on a plate. Dredge the shrimp to coat all sides in the mix.

2 In a skillet, heat olive oil over medium-high heat.

3 Carefully add the shrimp and cook 3 minutes on each side or until slightly browned. When done, set aside.

4 To assemble, place ¼ of the shrimp on the bottom half of the bread. Scoop ¼ cup of the coleslaw on top of the shrimp, followed by pickle slices, then the top half of the sandwich.

5 Serve immediately.

THE *PEACH* STADIUM

Georgia is well-known as the "Peach State," and Turner Field lives up to this fruity moniker. From the famous peach cobbler at 755 Club at Turner Field to locally made peach-flavored ice cream, sweet treats abound throughout the stadium. Afterward, work off calories at the kid-friendly game called the "Peach Pitch," located at the stadium's West Pavilion, where youngsters can test their skills by throwing peaches into baskets.

SWEET 'N' SPICY COLESLAW

PREP	COOK	MAKES
5 MINUTES	0 MINUTES	4 SERVINGS

INGREDIENTS

◇	1 cup	coleslaw mix
◇	2 tablespoons	mayonnaise
◇	1 tablespoon	sour cream
◇	1 tablespoon	apple cider vinegar
◇	2 teaspoons	hot sauce
◇	1 teaspoon	honey
◇	½ teaspoon	salt

1 Combine the coleslaw mix, mayonnaise, sour cream, apple cider vinegar, hot sauce, honey, and salt in a mixing bowl. Stir well.

2 Serve on Shrimp Po' Boys. Store leftovers in an airtight container in refrigerator for up to 3 days.

PEACH SMOOTHIE

PREP	COOK	MAKES
5 MINUTES	0 MINUTES	4 SMOOTHIES

INGREDIENTS

◇	1 cup	plain yogurt
◇	1 cup	milk
◇	2 cups	frozen peaches
◇	¼ cup	orange juice
◇	1 teaspoon	honey
◇	8	ice cubes

1 Combine all ingredients in a blender. Blend until smooth.

2 Pour into glasses for serving.

MIA

Miami Marlins Baseball Club

MARLINS PARK

LOCATION	
Miami, Florida	
OPENED	
2012	
CAPACITY	
36,742	

The Marlins joined the National League in 1993, making them one of the newest teams in Major League Baseball. And during their first years, they shared Sun Life Stadium with the NFL's Dolphins. While the bad weather doesn't stop a football game, it can be tough to get in nine innings with Florida's hot, humid, and rainy weather. So in 2012, the team moved into Marlins Park. It's currently the newest of all pro ballparks and features a retractable roof. It's a nice and cozy stadium — the smallest in baseball — and breaks from the trendy retro feel for a modern look with a steel and glass facade.

NACHO HELMET

with KEY LIMEADE

Being so close to the ocean, seafood is highly popular at Marlins Park. Add to that a thriving Central and South American populace, and you get specialties like ceviche, empanadas, and tamales. But for fans looking to fill their stomachs and take home a souvenir, the nacho helmet is the stadium's lead-off choice. Serve with Key limeade for a true taste of SoFlo.

NACHO HELMET

PREP	COOK	MAKES
5 MINUTES	**10** MINUTES	**4** HELMETS

INGREDIENTS

◇	1 pound	ground beef or turkey
◇	1 tablespoon	cumin
◇	1 tablespoon	chili powder
◇	1 teaspoon	paprika
◇	1 teaspoon	oregano
◇	1/4 teaspoon	cayenne pepper
◇	1 teaspoon	salt
◇	1/2 cup	water
◇	8 ounces	cheddar cheese
◇	1 15-ounce can	refried beans
◇	1 13-ounce bag	tortilla chips
◇	optional toppings: sour cream and	
◇	pico de gallo (see page 60)	

1 In a skillet over medium heat, brown the ground beef until no longer pink. Carefully drain fat.

2 Reduce heat to medium-low and add the cumin, chili powder, paprika, oregano, cayenne pepper, salt, and water. Bring to a simmer and cook for 10 minutes.

3 Meanwhile, grate the cheese and set aside.

4 Heat the refried beans in a saucepan over medium heat and set aside.

5 To assemble, spread the chips evenly in a helmet or on a platter. Pour the beans over the chips, followed by meat, cheese, and desired toppings.

6 Serve immediately.

HELMET HUNGER

The trend of serving food in batting helmets isn't new. In fact, ice cream sundae helmets were first served at ballparks in the early 1970s! The miniature plastic helmets quickly became fan collectables and an easy way for Major League teams to advertise their brands. Today, ice cream sundae helmets can be found at most MLB stadiums, but a few teams serve up megameals in full-sized batting helmets.

POUTINE HELMET
(Philadelphia Phillies, Citizens Bank Park)

Fries, cheese, bacon, and gravy served in plastic helmet.

KEY LIMEADE

PREP	COOK	MAKES
10	0	2
MINUTES	MINUTES	QUARTS

	INGREDIENTS	
◇	6 cups	water, divided
◇	1 ½ cups	granulated sugar
◇	2 cups	lime juice
◇	ice cubes and lime slices, for serving	
◇		

1 In a saucepan, combine 2 cups of water with the sugar and bring to a low boil over medium-high heat. Stir to dissolve the sugar, then remove from heat.

2 In a pitcher, combine the boiled sugar water, the other 4 cups of water, and lime juice. Stir well.

3 Serve in glasses with ice cubes and lime slices.

CHICHARRONES
(San Francisco Giants, AT&T Park)

Fried pork rinds served with chili-lime salt in a miniature plastic cap.

RIB BUCKET
(Chicago White Sox, U.S. Cellular Field)

Ribs, french fries, coleslaw, and cornbread served in a full-sized helmet.

NYM

New York Mets Baseball Club

CITI FIELD

LOCATION
Queens, New York
OPENED
2009
CAPACITY
41,922
NICKNAMES
New Shea

In the spring of 2009, the Mets moved from their original home, Shea Stadium, to the classically styled Citi Field. While a new ballpark, walking into Citi Field is like time traveling back to when the Dodgers and Giants dominated New York's playing fields. It's an old-fashioned, bowled-shaped park with red brick and limestone arches over the entrances. Nearly half of the seating is on the lower level, so fans can get an intimate view of the their favorite players. Of their two World Series, neither was won at Citi Field, but soon after the park opened, Mets outfielder Gary Sheffield blasted his 500th home run, and on June 1, 2012, pitcher Johan Santana threw the team's first ever no-hitter.

GARLIC FRIES

with CHOCOLATE-BANANA MILKSHAKE

Located in New York City's Queens borough, there are varied food options at Citi Field, from fried flounder to New York style pizza and Italian hero sandwiches. But one fave, garlic fries, is packed with nine innings worth of flavor. Pair them with a cool, creamy chocolate-banana milkshake for the perfect salty and sweet combination.

GARLIC FRIES

PREP	COOK	MAKES
10	**30**	**4**
MINUTES	MINUTES	SERVINGS

	INGREDIENTS	
◇	4	russet potatoes
◇	¼ cup	olive oil
◇	1 tablespoon	crushed garlic
◇	1 teaspoons	salt
◇	½ teaspoon	ground black pepper

1. Preheat oven to 450°F and line a baking sheet with parchment paper. Set aside.

2. Peel and cut the potatoes into ¼-inch wide sticks, like french fries. Dry well with a paper towel and place in mixing bowl with olive oil, crushed garlic, salt, and ground black pepper. Stir until the potatoes are coated.

3. Arrange the potatoes on the baking sheet and place in the oven for 15 minutes. Then flip them with a spatula and bake an additional 15 minutes or until golden brown and crispy.

4. Serve immediately.

Hall of Fame FOODIE

Relief pitcher **Turk Wendell** (New York Mets 1997–2001) might be one of the most superstitious players in MLB history. Between each inning, Wendell would brush his teeth and eat four sticks of licorice!

CHOCOLATE-BANANA MILKSHAKE

PREP	COOK	MAKES
10	**0**	**2**
MINUTES	MINUTES	SHAKES

	INGREDIENTS	
◇	2 cups	chocolate ice cream
◇	2	bananas, peeled
◇	½ cup	milk

1 Combine the ice cream, bananas, and milk in a blender. Blend until smooth.

2 Pour into glasses and serve cold.

New York City is known as the Big Apple, but Citi Field is home to one of the biggest apples in all of New York. The Home Run Apple (left), located in center field, stands sixteen-feet tall and weighs 4,800 pounds, significantly larger than the original apple from the old Shea Stadium (above) which is now on display outside Citi Field. When a Mets player hits a home run, the center-field apple lifts from its encasement and illuminates in celebration.

87

PHI

Philadelphia Phillies Baseball Club

CITIZENS BANK PARK

LOCATION	
Philadelphia, Pennsylvania	
OPENED	
2004	
CAPACITY	
43,651	
NICKNAMES	
The Bank	

Until the spring of 2004, the Phillies shared Veterans Stadium with the NFL's Eagles. But they joined many teams in the aughts that wanted wide-open, retro stadiums specifically for the baseball fan. Citizens Bank Park, the Phillies new home, is part of the South Philadelphia Sports Complex, which also includes the Eagles's new stadium, Lincoln Financial Field, and Wells Fargo Center, which hosts the NHL's Flyers and NBA's 76ers. Not only are the Phillies one of the MLB's oldest teams, having won two World Series (1980 and 2008), but the city itself is rich in history, housing the Liberty Bell at Independence Hall. Out in right-center field stands a 50-foot-tall replica of the Liberty Bell, and whenever a Philly slugs a home run, it swings and rings out.

PHILLY CHEESESTEAK SLIDERS

with CRABBY TOTS

The Philly cheesesteak is the signature sandwich of Philadelphia and the signature concession of Citizens Bank Park. With tender, juicy steak and melted mounds of cheese, there's a whole lot to love in this City of Brotherly Love classic. Pair them with these salty, seasoned tater tots, a fun twist on the stadium's famous Crabfries.

PHILLY CHEESESTEAK SLIDERS

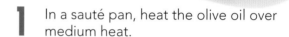

PREP	COOK	MAKES
20	**10**	**12**
MINUTES	MINUTES	SLIDERS

	INGREDIENTS	
◇	2 tablespoons	olive oil
◇	1 pound	London broil, sliced thinly
◇	½	onion, sliced thinly
◇	1	bell pepper, sliced thinly
◇	½ teaspoon	salt
◇	¼ teaspoon	black pepper
◇	½ cup	beef stock or broth
◇	12	slices provolone cheese
◇	12	slider buns

1 In a sauté pan, heat the olive oil over medium heat.

2 Add the sliced peppers and onions. Cook for about five minutes or until slightly softened.

3 Carefully add the meat without splattering. Stir well.

4 Add the beef stock or broth and turn the heat up to high.

5 Cook the meat for an additional 1–2 minutes or until most of the broth is evaporated. Set aside.

6 Open the slider buns and place them on a large sheet pan.

7 Using tongs, place an equal amount of meat, onion, and pepper on half of the buns.

8 Place a slice of cheese on top of the meat and place in the oven.

9 Turn on the broil function on the oven. Bake for about 3 minutes or until the cheese is melted and bubbly. Check often to avoid burning.

10 Place bun tops on the sandwiches and serve.

Hall of Fame FOODIE

Philadelphia-born **Jack Norworth** wrote baseball's seventh-inning stretch song, "Take Me Out to the Ball Game," which includes the popular lyric, "Buy me some peanuts and cracker Jack." These two snacks remain popular at baseball stadiums to this day.

CRABBY TOTS

PREP	COOK	MAKES
5	**30**	**4**
MINUTES	MINUTES	SERVINGS

	INGREDIENTS	
◇	1 pound	frozen tater tots
◇	1 tablespoon	olive oil
◇	2 tablespoons	Old Bay seasoning
◇		
◇		
◇		
◇		
◇		

1 Bake tater tots according to package directions on large baking sheet lined with parchment paper.

2 When the tots are done, place them into a large mixing bowl. Drizzle with olive oil and sprinkle with Old Bay seasoning and toss gently.

3 Serve immediately. Dip in cheesy dipping sauce (see page 99), if desired.

THE GREAT CHEESESTEAK DEBATE

Brothers Pat and Harry Olivieri, the founders of Pat's King of Steaks, served up the first Philly cheesesteak more than 85 years ago. There's no debating their history, but the city's favorite sandwich is the subject of heated arguments. In 1966, Joey Vento opened Geno's Steaks across the street. The two competing sandwich shops have been rivals ever since. Although their cheesesteaks are similar, one ingredient sets them apart: cheese! Pat's prefers Cheez Whiz while Geno's tops their sandwiches with provolone. Either way, food lovers can't lose.

VS.

WAS

Washington Nationals Baseball Club

NATIONALS PARK

LOCATION
Washington, DC
OPENED
2008
CAPACITY
41,418

For more than 30 years, the nation's capital was without a baseball team. But that all changed in 2005, when the Montreal Expos relocated to Washington, DC, and switched names to the Nationals. A few years later, in 2008, Nationals Park opened. Unlike many new ball fields that try to capture those bygone days with a classic brick look, the Nationals's stadium has a sleek, modern feel with a glass and steel facade. From the stadium's upper deck, fans can glimpse the US Capitol Building.

CHILI CHEESE FRIES

with KETTLE CORN

Being the seat of the US government, DC attracts people from all over the world, so it's only fitting that Nationals Park offers a wide variety of food choices, from sushi to burritos, shawarmas, and more, representing the area's many ethnicities. But for fans who want that iconic Nationals Park treat, it's chili smothering hot dogs, spaghetti, nachos, or fries

CHILI CHEESE FRIES

PREP	COOK	MAKES
10 MINUTES	**30** MINUTES	**4** SERVINGS

	INGREDIENTS	
◇	4	russet potatoes
◇	¼ cup	olive oil
◇	1 teaspoon	salt
◇	½ teaspoon	ground black pepper
◇	4 ounces	cheddar cheese
◇	1 recipe	chili from Coney Dogs (see page 42)
◇		

1 Preheat oven to 450°F and line a baking sheet with parchment paper. Set aside.

2 Peel and cut the potatoes into ¼-inch wide sticks, like french fries. Dry well with a paper towel and place in mixing bowl with olive oil, salt, and ground black pepper. Stir until the potatoes are coated.

3 Arrange the potatoes on the baking sheet and place in the oven for 15 minutes, then flip them with a spatula and bake an additional 15 minutes or until golden brown and crispy.

4 To assemble, place fries on a plate, followed by chili, and sprinkle with cheese.

5 Serve immediately.

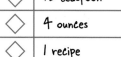

EVERY DAY IS FRY DAY!

There are enough french fry varieties throughout the Major Leagues for a whole week of fry days.

MONDAY	TUESDAY	WEDNESDAY
Chili Cheese Fries at Nationals Park (Washington Nationals)	**Garlic Fries at Citi Field** (New York Mets)	**Poutine Fries at Rogers Centre** (Toronto Blue Jays)

KETTLE CORN

PREP	COOK	MAKES
5 MINUTES	5 MINUTES	4 SERVINGS

	INGREDIENTS	
◇	¼ cup	oil
◇	¼ cup	granulated sugar
◇	½ cup	popping corn

1 In a saucepan over medium-high heat, add the oil and sugar. When the oil is hot, add the popping corn and place the lid on top of the saucepan.

2 When the corn begins popping, start sliding the pan over the burner back and forth to keep the sugar from burning.

3 Pop the corn for about 2 minutes or until the popping slows down. Continue sliding the pan for another minute or two before transferring to a serving bowl.

4 Serve immediately. Store leftovers in an airtight container at room temperature for up to 1 day.

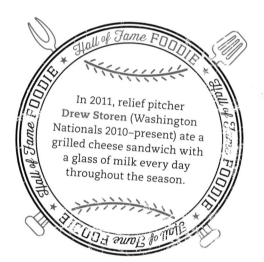

Hall of Fame FOODIE

In 2011, relief pitcher **Drew Storen** (Washington Nationals 2010–present) ate a grilled cheese sandwich with a glass of milk every day throughout the season.

THURSDAY	FRIDAY	SATURDAY	SUNDAY
Disco Fries at Yankee Stadium (New York Yankees)	**Carne Asada Fries at Petco Park** (San Diego Padres)	**Crabfries at Citizens Bank Park** (Philadelphia Phillies)	**Plain French Fries, available everywhere!**

CHC

Chicago Cubs Baseball Club

WRIGLEY FIELD

LOCATION
Chicago, Illinois
OPENED
1914
CAPACITY
41,160
NICKNAMES
The Friendly Confines
Cubs Park

When it comes to pure history and atmosphere, few ballparks can compete with the "friendly confines" of Wrigley Field. Built in 1914, this gem on the north side of Chicago has been home to more than a century of professional baseball. Wrigley's outfield fence — brick covered with thick green ivy — is its hallmark. By modern standards, the stadium is small, seating just more than 40,000. But some of the most prized seating isn't even in the stadium, as adjacent buildings offer fans "rooftop seating" that allows them to look in on ball games without ever entering the park!

PRETZEL TWISTS

with HONEY MUSTARD & CHEESY DIPPING SAUCES

Whether inside the stadium or in the streets of surrounding Wrigleyville, fans have a wide range of food choices. From juicy Chicago-style hot dogs and deep-dish pizza to Wrigley's famous giant twist pretzel, complete with cheesy dipping sauce. The food on the north side of Chicago is hearty and delicious.

PRETZEL TWISTS

PREP	COOK	MAKES
1¼ MINUTES	30 MINUTES	6 TWISTS

INGREDIENTS

◇	1 packet	instant yeast
◇	2 tablespoons	salt
◇	1 teaspoon	honey
◇	1 cup	warm water
◇	2 ½ cups	flour, plus more for kneading
◇	3 cups	water
◇	½ cup	baking soda
◇		vegetable oil spray
◇	6 tablespoons	melted butter
◇	optional sprinklings: kosher salt, poppy seeds,	
◇	sesame seeds	

1 In a large mixing bowl, combine the yeast, salt, honey, and warm water. Allow to sit 2 minutes.

2 Add the flour. Mix well and turn the bowl onto a floured surface. Knead the dough well with your hands for about 5 minutes, or until it is soft and smooth.

3 Spray the inside of a clean mixing bowl with vegetable oil spray and place the dough in the bowl. Cover with a clean damp cloth and allow to sit for 30 minutes to rise.

4 Flour a surface and place the dough on it. Knead 1 minute, then cut the dough into 6 pieces.

5 Roll the dough between your hands and the counter to make ropes about 12 inches long.

6 Fold a rope in half and then twist it to make the dough braided. Repeat for remaining dough and set aside.

7 Preheat your oven to 400°F. Spray the baking sheet with a light coating of vegetable oil spray.

8 Boil water in a saucepan. Add baking soda and stir until it dissolves. Reduce the heat so it slowly simmers. Drop the twists in the saucepan two at a time. Let them cook for 30 seconds.

9 Place the twists ¼-inch apart on the baking sheet. Sprinkle with salt and seeds, if desired.

10 Bake for 15 minutes or until golden brown. Then brush with melted butter before serving.

Hall of Fame FOODIE

Legend has it that former pitcher **Lee Smith** (Chicago Cubs 1980–87) always slept through the first four innings of games that he pitched. As instructed, his teammates would wake him up with a cheeseburger before the fifth inning started.

HONEY-MUSTARD DIPPING SAUCE

PREP	COOK	MAKES
5	**0**	**1 ½**
MINUTES	MINUTES	CUPS

	INGREDIENTS	
◇	1 cup	coarse ground mustard
◇	1/2 cup	honey
◇	1 teaspoon	salt
◇		

1 Combine all of the ingredients in a mixing bowl.

2 Taste the mixture and add more honey or mustard if needed. Serve alongside your pretzel twists.

CHEESY DIPPING SAUCE

PREP	COOK	MAKES
5	**5**	**1**
MINUTES	MINUTES	CUP

	INGREDIENTS	
◇	2 ounces	sharp cheddar cheese
◇	1 tablespoon	butter
◇	1 tablespoon	all-purpose flour
◇	1 cup	milk
◇	½ teaspoon	salt
◇	½ teaspoon	paprika
◇		

1 Grate the cheese and set aside. In a saucepan over medium heat, melt the butter and add the flour. Whisk gently until the flour absorbs the butter.

2 Slowly pour in the milk while whisking quickly.

3 As the liquid thickens, add the cheese, salt, and paprika, stirring frequently until the cheese completely melts.

4 Pour into a serving bowl and serve immediately.

CIN

Cincinnati Reds Baseball Club

GREAT AMERICAN BALL PARK

LOCATION
Cincinnati, Ohio
OPENED
2003
CAPACITY
42,319
NICKNAMES
GABP

With a name like the Great American Ball Park, you'd expect a lot out of the Cincinnati Reds's home. And it doesn't disappoint. At 40 feet tall and 138 feet wide, the GABP can brag about having one of the largest HD scoreboards in baseball and is that classic, bowl-shaped ballpark that today's fans love in their home fields. The Reds began playing ball at GABP in 2003, with Reds superstar Ken Griffey Jr. getting the first hit, a double. The Reds are one of the oldest teams, joining the National League way back in 1882. And fans take pride in their team's history, which includes five World Series wins. The Reds Hall of Fame Museum sits next door to the park and at GABP's main entrance is Crosely Terrace, where fans are greeted by statues of great players from bygone days, including Frank Robinson, Ted Kluszewski, and Johnny Bench.

CINCINNATI-STYLE CHILI

with COLOSSAL COOKIE SUNDAE

If you're hungry, there are few better parks to fill up in, starting with topped fries. They can come covered in smoked chicken, pulled pork, or cheese and hot sauce. Cincinnati is also renowned for its chili, and it's used to cover everything from fries to spaghetti.

CINCINNATI-STYLE CHILI

PREP	COOK	MAKES
15 MINUTES	30 MINUTES	4 SERVINGS

INGREDIENTS

◇	1	small onion
◇	1 tablespoon	olive oil
◇	1 pound	ground beef or turkey
◇	1 15-ounce can	tomato sauce
◇	1 ½ cups	beef broth
◇	4 tablespoons	chili powder
◇	1 teaspoon	cumin
◇	¼ teaspoon	allspice
◇	¼ teaspoon	ground cloves
◇	½ teaspoon	ground cinnamon
◇	1 teaspoon	unsweetened cocoa powder
◇	½ teaspoon	paprika
◇	1 tablespoon + 1 teaspoon	salt, divided
◇	8 ounces	spaghetti noodles
◇	8 ounces	cheddar cheese
◇		
◇		
◇		
◇		
◇		
◇		
◇		

1 Chop the onion into small pieces and set aside.

2 In a medium-sized pot, heat the olive oil over medium heat. Add the onions and stir occasionally for about 5 minutes or until they begin to soften.

3 Add the meat, breaking it up with a spoon as it cooks.

4 When the meat has browned, add the tomato sauce, beef broth, chili powder, cumin, allspice, ground cloves, ground cinnamon, cocoa powder, paprika, and 1 teaspoon salt. Stir to combine and bring to a simmer.

5 Reduce heat to medium-low and simmer for 20 minutes, stirring occasionally.

6 Meanwhile, fill a large pot with water and add 1 tablespoon salt. Place on a burner over high heat until it begins to boil. Add the pasta and cook until just tender, about 8 minutes. Drain through a colander. Set aside.

7 Grate the cheese and set aside. To assemble, place some pasta on a plate, followed by 1 cup of the chili, and sprinkle with ¼ cup cheese. Serve immediately.

COLOSSAL COOKIE SUNDAE

PREP	COOK	MAKES
5 MINUTES	**0** MINUTES	**1** SUNDAE

	INGREDIENTS	
◇	3 scoops	cookie dough ice cream
◇	3	chocolate–vanilla crème
◇		sandwich cookies
◇	¼ cup	chocolate syrup
◇	¼ cup	caramel sauce
◇	1	maraschino cherry

1 Place the scoops of ice cream in a bowl.

2 Crumble the cookies in your hands and sprinkle over the ice cream.

3 Drizzle the sauces over the top, followed by cherry. Serve immediately.

CHILI CAPITAL OF THE WORLD

Cincinnati is sometimes referred to as the "Chili Capital of the World." More than 250 chili restaurants operate throughout the city, and residents consume more than two million pounds of chili annually! In the early 20th century, Macedonian and Greek immigrants arrived in New York. Some entrepreneurs opened hot dog stands, topping their specialty dogs with Turkish-spiced chili. The chili dogs, later known as Coney Dogs, made their way to the Midwest, from Cincinnati to Detroit. Eventually, the chili itself made its way atop a pile of spaghetti, the origins of which are often disputed. Unlike Texas-style chili, beans are not included, while sweet and spicy flavors of cloves, cinnamon, and cocoa dominate the chili's unique flavor.

MILLER PARK

LOCATION	
Milwaukee, Wisconsin	
OPENED	
2001	
CAPACITY	
41,900	

In the spring of 2001, the Brewers joined the handful of teams playing in a stadium with a retractable roof. And like the team itself, Miller Stadium is named after one of Milwaukee's most famous industries: Miller Brewing Company. The stadium showcases a huge scoreboard in center field, and over in left field is Bernie's Dugout, home of the Brewer's mascot. Every time a Brewer slams a home run, Bernie celebrates by sliding down from his perch. Walking through the home plate entrance, fans are greeted by statues of some of the greats to don a Brewer uniform, like Robin Yount and Hank Aaron, as well as longtime radio announcer Bob Uecker.

BRATWURST SLIDERS

with CHEESE PUFFS

Along with the brewing industry, Wisconsin is known for cheese and bratwurst. And both come in abundance at Miller Stadium, from fried cheese curds to the 18-inch Down Wisconsin Avenue Brat. To take their love of sausages even further, the sixth inning features a Sausage Race, in which five people in sausage costumes run around the park

BRATWURST SLIDERS

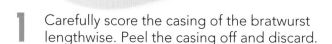

PREP	COOK	MAKES
30 MINUTES	**10** MINUTES	**12** SLIDERS

INGREDIENTS		
◇	6	fresh bratwursts
◇	1	onion
◇	1 tablespoon	olive oil
◇	1 teaspoon	salt
◇	½ teaspoon	black pepper
◇	12	pretzel slider buns
◇ ◇	optional toppings: honey-mustard dipping sauce (see page 99) and/or sauerkraut	

1 Carefully score the casing of the bratwurst lengthwise. Peel the casing off and discard.

2 Cut each sausage link in half. Use your hands to form the meat into patties.

3 Slice the onion thinly and set aside. Heat olive oil in a large skillet over medium heat and add the sliced onions. Stir, then sprinkle a little salt and pepper in the pan. Cook until the onions are softened and slightly golden brown. Remove from pan and set aside.

4 Using the same pan, turn the heat to medium and add the bratwurst patties, working in batches if necessary. Cook for about 3–4 minutes per side, or until each side is browned and cooked in the middle.

5 Open the pretzel bun and place a bratwurst burger on the bottom. Add about 2 tablespoons of onion. You can also add sauerkraut on top of the onions.

6 Spread 1 tablespoon of the honey mustard on the inside of the top half of the pretzel bun. Place the top half of the bun on top and serve on a platter.

TOP SAUSAGE

Miller Park is the only Major League ballpark where sausages — including brats and Polish and Italian sausages — outsell hot dogs! Sausage sales are nearly double the sales of hot dogs annually.

CHEESE PUFFS

PREP	COOK	MAKES
5	20	1
MINUTES	MINUTES	QUART

INGREDIENTS	
1 17.3-ounce package	frozen puff pastry, thawed
32	cheese curds
1	egg
2 tablespoons	cool water

Hall of Fame FOODIE

Before each start, pitcher **Matt Garza** (Milwaukee Brewers 2014–present) eats the same fried chicken meal before every game. In fact, he orders fried chicken for the entire team on game day!

1. Preheat oven to 400°F and line a baking sheet with parchment paper. Set aside.

2. Begin cutting the first pastry sheet by slicing it into 16 equal squares. Repeat for the second sheet.

3. Place a cheese curd in the lower right corner of each square.

4. Whisk the egg in a mixing bowl with the water.

5. Brush the egg wash onto the edges of the squares on all sides.

6. Starting from the right corner, start rolling dough over the cheese curd, folding in the sides as you roll. Press the edges to seal and set on the baking sheet. Repeat for the rest of the squares.

7. Brush the remaining egg wash on top of the dough and place in the oven for 20 minutes, check on them after 15 minutes.

8. When they are golden brown, remove from the oven and allow to cool for about 5 minutes before serving.

PIT

Pittsburgh Pirates Baseball Club

PNC PARK

LOCATION
Pittsburgh, Pennsylvania
OPENED
2001
CAPACITY
38,362
NICKNAMES
The Park

For 30 years, the Pirates shared a stadium with the NFL's Steelers. But like many other teams in the aughts, they moved to a park dedicated solely to baseball. PNC Park opened in the spring of 2001. The Pirates are one of the oldest teams in baseball, joining the National League in 1882. In their more than 100-year history, they've won five World Series. But the new park hasn't brought them any luck yet. While a Pittsburgh native, Sean Casey, got the park's first hit, a home run over right-center, he was playing for the Reds at the time. PNC Park is one of the smallest ballparks, seating just fewer than 40,000 fans. Still, it is worth visiting for the amazing views of the Pittsburgh skyline and the Roberto Clemente Bridge, named after one of the team's greats.

SPICY PITTSBURGH-STYLE SANDWICH

with PEANUT BUTTER CUP FUDGE

Pittsburgh is known for its hard-working, blue-collar folks, and what better reward for a long day on the job than a hearty sandwich? The city's favorite sandwich shop, Primanti Brothers, has dozens of restaurants across Pennsylvania, including inside PNC Park. This Pittsburgh-style sandwich is stuffed with meat, coleslaw, and french fries.

SPICY PITTSBURGH-STYLE SANDWICH

PREP	COOK	MAKES
5 MINUTES	30 MINUTES	4 SANDWICHES

INGREDIENTS

◇	2 cups	frozen french fries
◇	1	French bread loaf
◇	1 pound	sliced hot capicola ham
◇	8	slices provolone cheese
◇	8	leaves lettuce
◇	4 tablespoons	mayonnaise, divided

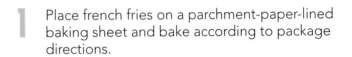

1 Place french fries on a parchment-paper-lined baking sheet and bake according to package directions.

2 Meanwhile, cut the French bread into 4 equal pieces, then slice horizontally.

3 Place the meat in a large skillet over medium-high heat. Turn the meat frequently to prevent sticking.

4 When the meat is slightly browned, divide it equally among the bottom halves of the four sandwiches.

5 Top with provolone cheese, ½ cup of french fries, and 2 lettuce leaves.

6 Spread 1 tablespoon of mayonnaise on each of the top halves and place on top of the sandwiches. Serve immediately.

KETCHUP KING

Baseball and hot dogs go hand in hand, and some believe hot dogs and ketchup do too! Ketchup devotees owe a lot to Pittsburgh. The city is home to Heinz, maker of America's bestselling ketchup. In fact, Heinz Stadium is home to Pittsburgh's other beloved sports team, the Steelers.

PEANUT BUTTER CUP FUDGE

PREP	COOK	MAKES
10	**4**	**16**
MINUTES	HOURS	PIECES

INGREDIENTS

◇	2 tablespoons	unsalted butter, divided
◇	1 14-ounce can	sweetened condensed
◇		milk, divided
◇	2 cups	semisweet chocolate chips
◇	1 cup	peanut butter chips
◇	generous sprays	cooking spray

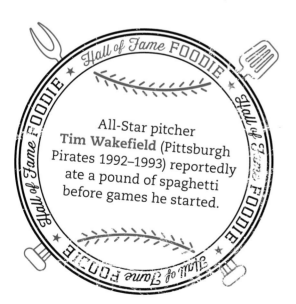

All-Star pitcher **Tim Wakefield** (Pittsburgh Pirates 1992–1993) reportedly ate a pound of spaghetti before games he started.

1 Generously spray a baking dish with cooking spray and set aside.

2 In a microwave-safe bowl, combine 1 ½ tablespoons butter, 1 ¼ cups sweetened condensed milk, and the semisweet chocolate chips. Microwave at 50% power for 30 seconds. Stir with a spatula and microwave for an additional 30 seconds or until the chocolate is melted and smooth.

3 Pour the mixture in the baking dish and spread evenly.

4 Working quickly, combine ½ tablespoon butter, ½ cup sweetened condensed milk, and the peanut butter chips in a second microwave-safe bowl. Microwave at 50% power for 30 seconds. Stir with a spatula and microwave for an additional 30 seconds or until chips are melted and smooth.

5 Pour the mixture over the top of the chocolate and spread evenly. Place in refrigerator for at least 4 hours.

6 To serve, cut into 16 squares. Serve cooled or at room temperature. Store leftovers in an airtight container in refrigerator for up to 1 week.

STL

St. Louis Cardinals Baseball Club

BUSCH STADIUM

LOCATION
St. Louis, Missouri
OPENED
2006
CAPACITY
43,975
NICKNAMES
Busch Stadium III

The Cardinals must really like the name of their stadium because every park in which they have played has been called "Busch Stadium." They were all named after Gussie Busch who bought the team in 1953. The latest incarnation of Busch Stadium opened in April 2006, so it is one of the newest stadiums in baseball. But its grass field and openness give it a classic baseball feel. Which is only fitting, as over the outfield wall, fans get a view of the Gateway Arch, a landmark as iconically American as baseball. The Cardinals quickly put their stadium to good use, winning a World Series the same year it opened, and then one more in 2011.

TOASTED RAVIOLI

with MARINARA SAUCE

Every ballpark has its signature food — the one thing every fan and visitor must try to make their visit complete. At Busch Stadium, that's toasted ravioli and toasted cannelloni. These crispy treats are stuffed with meat and cheese, and then fans dip them in steamy

TOASTED RAVIOLI

PREP	COOK	MAKES
10	5	4
MINUTES	MINUTES	SERVINGS

	INGREDIENTS	
◇	1 cup	all-purpose flour
◇	2	eggs
◇	1 cup	Italian-seasoned
◇		bread crumbs
◇	16	refrigerated raviolis
◇	½ cup	olive oil
◇	1 recipe	marinara sauce
◇		

1 Create your breading station: place flour on 1 plate, eggs on a second plate, and bread crumbs on a third. Whisk the eggs with a fork.

2 Roll a ravioli in the flour, then dip in egg, letting the excess drip off. Finally, roll the ravioli in the bread crumbs. Set on a plate or cutting board. Repeat for the rest of the raviolis.

3 In a skillet, heat the olive oil over medium heat.

4 When the oil is hot, carefully place about 4 raviolis in the skillet.

5 Cook for about 2 minutes or until golden brown. Carefully turn the raviolis over to cook the other side for an additional 2 minutes.

6 Transfer to a paper-towel-lined plate to drain.

7 Repeat in batches.

8 Serve hot with marinara sauce for dipping.

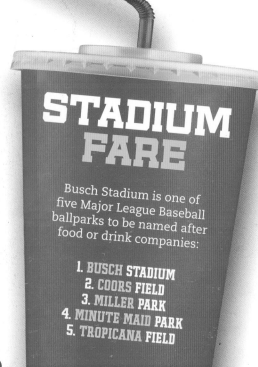

STADIUM FARE

Busch Stadium is one of five Major League Baseball ballparks to be named after food or drink companies:

1. BUSCH STADIUM
2. COORS FIELD
3. MILLER PARK
4. MINUTE MAID PARK
5. TROPICANA FIELD

MARINARA SAUCE

PREP	COOK	MAKES
5 MINUTES	10 MINUTES	1 SERVING

	INGREDIENTS	
◇	1 teaspoon	olive oil
◇	1 teaspoon	crushed garlic
◇	¼ teaspoon	crushed red pepper
◇		flakes
◇	8 ounces	crushed tomatoes
◇	1 teaspoon	salt
◇	1 teaspoon	sugar
◇	1 teaspoon	dried basil

1 In a skillet, heat the olive oil over medium heat.

2 Add garlic and red pepper flakes. Stir and cook for 1 minute.

3 Pour the crushed tomatoes in the skillet, along with the salt, sugar, and basil.

4 Bring to a simmer and cook for 10 minutes.

LEGENDARY *Pasta*

St. Louis's Most Valuable Pasta has Hall of Fame origins! Toasted ravioli originated in a part of the city called The Hill, sometime called "America's Other Little Italy." Two Major League catchers, future Hall-of-Famer Yogi Berra and Joe Garagiola (St. Louis Cardinals 1946–1951), grew up on The Hill as neighbors and young competitors, both entering professional baseball in 1946. In fact, one legend says that Garagiola's older brother, Mickey Garagiola, was working as a waiter on the day toasted ravioli was first made. On that day, a chef accidently dropped ravioli into boiling oil instead of boiling water. Instead of throwing them away, the chef served them up, and a St. Louis favorite was born!

ARI

Arizona Diamondbacks Baseball Club

CHASE FIELD

LOCATION
Phoenix, Arizona
OPENED
1998
CAPACITY
48,519
NICKNAMES
The BOB
The Snake Pit
The Aircraft Hangar

The Diamondbacks are one of the youngest teams in the MLB, joining the National League in 1998. So of course they had to have one of the best and largest scoreboards, standing 47 feet tall, and one of the coolest stadiums in the league. And they literally needed it. On those sunny summer days, Arizona's sweltering heat would be unbearable for players and fans alike. Chase Field was the first baseball park to have both a retractable roof, which is closed during those hot day games and open for the cooler night games, and a grass field. The cool, new stadium must have been lucky for the Diamondbacks. Shortly after entering the MLB, they won a World Series (2001). And no wonder, they had the Big Unit, Randy Johnson, on the mound that year.

ARIZONA HOT DOG

with SOPAIPILLAS

A trendy new stadium deserves some trendy new eats. So think food trucks. Food Truck Alley features different food trucks every game, with many eats having a southwestern flare. For fans with a sweet tooth, there is the churro dog, topped with frozen yogurt

ARIZONA HOT DOG

PREP	COOK	MAKES
15 MINUTES	5 MINUTES	4 DOGS

INGREDIENTS

◇	4	slices bacon
◇	1	small tomato
◇	1	small onion
◇	4 ounces	cheddar cheese
◇	4	hot dog buns
◇	4 tablespoons	salsa verde, divided
◇	4 teaspoons	mayonnaise, divided
◇	1 teaspoon	hot sauce, divided

1. In a skillet over medium heat, fry the bacon until crisp. Remove and set aside.

2. In a second skillet, add hot dogs and 3 cups water. Simmer over medium heat for 5 minutes or until hot.

3. While the hot dogs are cooking, chop the onion and tomato into small pieces and set aside.

4. Grate the cheese and set aside.

5. To assemble the hot dogs, place hot dogs in the buns, followed by a slice of bacon on each. Sprinkle 1 tablespoon of tomato, followed by 1 tablespoon onion, 1 tablespoon salsa verde, and drizzle 1 teaspoon mayonnaise, and a ¼ teaspoon hot sauce on each hot dog. Top with cheese before serving.

The popularity of mobile food trucks has exploded across the country, and the Arizona Diamondbacks are capitalizing on this trend — to the benefit of hungry fans! On weekends, a rotating schedule of Phoenix's all-star food trucks park just outside Gate A at Chase Field. With local options from grilled cheese sandwiches to quesadillas to signature burgers, Diamondback fans never have to eat the same thing twice!

SOPAIPILLAS

PREP	COOK	MAKES
5	**5**	**4**
MINUTES	MINUTES	PIECES

INGREDIENTS

◇	4	small flour tortillas
◇	½ cup	granulated sugar
◇	2 teaspoons	ground cinnamon
◇	4 tablespoons	oil

1 Cut the tortillas into wedges. Set aside.

2 In a mixing bowl, combine the sugar and cinnamon. Stir well and set aside.

3 In a skillet, heat the oil over medium-high heat.

4 Working in batches, add some tortillas. Cook for about 30 seconds and turn over carefully with a tongs. Cook an additional 30 seconds.

5 Carefully remove from the hot oil to a space lined with paper towels to drain.

6 Allow to cool slightly before dipping in the cinnamon sugar.

7 Serve warm. Store leftovers in an airtight container at room temperature for up to 1 day.

What's the Count?

The United States Department of Agriculture recommends a daily intake of 2,640 calories for men and 1,785 calories for women. So what's the calorie count on some baseball classics?

Foot-long Hot Dog	
Calories	475
Cotton Candy	
Calories	225
Corn Dog	
Calories	450
Peanuts (1 ounce)	
Calories	125
Soft Pretzel	
Calories	390

COL

Colorado Rockies Baseball Club

COORS FIELD

LOCATION
Denver, Colorado
OPENED
1995
CAPACITY
50,398
NICKNAMES
Jurassic Park

In 1991, the Colorado Rockies were selected to be one of two expansion teams to join the MLB. The team initially shared Mile High Stadium with the NFL's Broncos until Coors Field opened in the spring of 1995. With the thin mountain air, the park is known as a hitters park, in which sluggers like Todd Helton, Larry Walker, and Carlos Gonzalez have thrived. The Rockies' stadium is built in downtown Denver, but to keep it from towering over nearby buildings, Coors Field is set 21 feet below street level. A purple row of seats wrapping around the stadium — twenty rows up on the upper deck — marks one mile above sea level.

ROCKY MOUNTAIN BURRITO

with CHOCOLATY BERRY KABOBS

Coors Field is said to have one of the best burgers in baseball, the Helton burger, named after one of the team's most-beloved players. Hot dogs are taken to a new level at Xtreme Dog, whose dogs are topped with everything from bacon to chili sauce. But those looking to stuff themselves look no further than this overstuffed Rocky Mountain Burrito!

ROCKY MOUNTAIN BURRITOS

PREP	COOK	MAKES
5 MINUTES	**30** MINUTES	**4** BURRITOS

INGREDIENTS

◇	generous sprays	cooking spray
◇	1	medium onion
◇	1 tablespoon	olive oil
◇	1 pound	lean ground beef or
◇		turkey
◇	2 teaspoons	crushed garlic
◇	1 teaspoon	salt
◇	1 teaspoon	cumin
◇	2 teaspoons	chili powder
◇	1 teaspoon	smoked paprika
◇	1 8-ounce can	diced green chiles,
◇		drained
◇	1 8-ounce can	Mexican tomato sauce
◇	1 15-ounce can	pinto beans in chili sauce
◇	8 ounces	Monterey Jack cheese
◇	4 burrito-sized	flour tortillas
◇ ◇	optional toppings: guacamole (see page 65), sour cream, and salsa	
◇		
◇		

1 Preheat oven to 425°F. Spray baking dish with cooking spray and set aside.

2 Chop the onion into small pieces and place in a skillet with olive oil over medium heat. Cook for about 5 minutes, stirring occasionally.

3 Add meat, breaking up gently with a spoon as it cooks.

4 When the meat is browned, add the crushed garlic, salt, cumin, chili powder, smoked paprika, diced green chiles, Mexican tomato sauce, and pinto beans.

5 Bring to a simmer and reduce heat to medium-low. Simmer for about 15 minutes.

6 While the filling simmers, grate the cheese and set aside.

7 When the filling is simmered, scoop out about 1 cup of the filling into each of the tortillas, then roll up, folding in the sides as well. Place them seam-side down in the baking dish.

8 Pour the remaining filling over the top of the burritos, then sprinkle with the cheese.

9 Place in the oven for about 10 minutes or until slightly browned.

10 Serve hot with fixings such as guacamole, sour cream, or salsa.

CHOCOLATY BERRY KABOBS

PREP	COOK	MAKES
10 MINUTES	0 MINUTES	8 KABOBS

INGREDIENTS	
◇ 6	large strawberries
◇ 24	blueberries
◇ 24	raspberries
◇ 2 ounces	chocolate almond bark

1 Place a large sheet of parchment paper on a flat surface.

2 Cut the tops off of each strawberry, then cut in quarters. Set aside.

3 Thread each skewer with 1 blueberry, followed by a raspberry, then a strawberry. Repeat 2 more times on each skewer.

4 Place finished skewers on parchment paper and set aside.

5 In a microwave-safe dish, heat the chocolate almond bark in the microwave at 50% power in 30 second increments until melted, stirring in between.

6 When the chocolate is melted, dip a fork in the chocolate and drizzle all over the kabobs.

7 Allow chocolate to cool before serving.

MILE-HIGH MEALS

Playing baseball at 5,280 feet is not without its difficulties. In 2002, the Colorado Rockies installed a humidor at Coors Field. The team stores baseballs inside the humidor to combat Denver's low humidity, which can make baseballs travel farther. Keeping baseballs at a constant 70 degrees and 50 percent humidity has helped reduce the relatively high number of home runs at the stadium.

When cooking at high elevations, chefs have to switch up their game plan too! At a mile above sea level, water boils at a lower temperature, so steamed or boiled foods take longer to cook. Baked goods often rise quickly, then fall. To combat this, increase baking temperatures by 15–25 degrees Fahrenheit.

LAD

Los Angeles Dodgers Baseball Club

DODGER STADIUM

LOCATION
Los Angeles, California
OPENED
1962
CAPACITY
56,000
NICKNAMES
Chavez Ravine
Blue Heaven On Earth

Along with the Giants, the Dodgers left New York in 1958 to find a new home in sunny California. Soon after, the city of Los Angeles had a new stadium built for their new baseball team. Opening April 10, 1962, Dodger Stadium is the third oldest MLB park currently in use. That means a lot of baseball history has happened here, including four of the Dodgers' six World Series titles. And some of the sport's greatest players have called Dodger Stadium home at one point during their careers, including pitchers Sandy Koufax and Don Sutton, and catcher Mike Piazza.

SOCAL HOT DOG

with MEXICAN CORN ON THE COB & BERRY-GRAPE COOLER

Like the local culture, the area's food is influenced by a large Hispanic population. Elote, Mexican corn on the cob with cheese and chili, is a must try to complete any Dodger Stadium experience. Carne asada nachos served in a plastic helmet is another fan fave. However, the simple yet uniquely sized, 10-inch hot dog is Dodger Stadium's bestseller.

SOCAL HOT DOG

PREP	COOK	MAKES
5 MINUTES	5 MINUTES	4 DOGS

	INGREDIENTS	
◇	4	hot dogs
◇	4 tablespoons	sweet pickle relish,
◇		divided
◇	4 teaspoons	yellow mustard
◇	4	hot dog buns

1 In a skillet, add the hot dogs with 3 cups water. Heat to simmering over medium heat. Cook for 5 minutes or until hot.

2 To assemble hot dog, place a hot dog in a bun, followed by 1 tablespoon of sweet pickle relish. Drizzle 1 teaspoon yellow mustard on top. Repeat for remaining hot dogs.

CITY OF HOT DOGS

In 2015, the National Hot Dog and Sausage Council predicted that Dodger Stadium would sell more hot dogs than any other Major League park. The more than 2.5 million hot dogs puts Dodger fans one million dogs above the next closest ballpark, Yankee Stadium. Most hot dogs sold at Dodger Stadium are "Dodger Dogs," a beloved 10-inch frankfurter that remains as simple and classic as when it was introduced in 1962.

MEXICAN CORN ON THE COB

PREP	COOK	MAKES
5	10	8
MINUTES	MINUTES	PIECES

	INGREDIENTS	
◇	8 ears	frozen sweet corn
◇	4 ounces	Mexican cheese, such
◇		as cotija
◇	8 tablespoons	mayonnaise, divided
◇	optional sprinklings: salt, pepper, and paprika	
◇		
◇		

1 Fill a large pot with water and bring to a boil. Add corn and reduce heat to simmering. Cook until tender, about 8 minutes.

2 Meanwhile, grate the cheese and set aside.

3 When the corn is cooked, remove carefully with a tongs. Allow to cool slightly before finishing, about 2 minutes.

4 Carefully spread 1 tablespoon of mayonnaise on each ear of corn. Sprinkle cheese generously all over the corn, followed by a dash of salt, pepper, and paprika. Serve hot.

BERRY-GRAPE COOLER

PREP	COOK	MAKES
5	0	2
MINUTES	MINUTES	QUARTS

	INGREDIENTS	
◇	2 cups	mixed berry juice
◇	2 cups	grape juice
◇	1 quart	lemon–lime soda
◇		ice cubes

1 In a pitcher, combine the mixed berry juice, grape juice, and lemon-lime soda. Stir well.

2 Serve in glasses with ice cubes.

San Diego Padres Baseball Club

PETCO PARK

LOCATION
San Diego, California
OPENED
2004
CAPACITY
41,164

The Padres shared a stadium with the NFL's Chargers until the opening of the 2004 season. That spring, they began playing in Petco Park, and celebrated their new-home opener with a win over in-state rivals, the Giants. Initially considered a great pitchers park — Trevor Hoffman threw a record-setting 500th career save here on June 6, 2007 — the outfield walls have since been moved in to help batters. The stadium captures the near-tropic feel of Southern California. The area around the park is landscaped with jacaranda and palm trees, and the main walkway up to the park has a stairway waterfall. Just outside the park's center-field wall is "Park at the Park," a grassy area where families can sit on blankets and view a game as if they were hanging out in their own backyards.

FISH TACOS

with CHIPOTLE MAYO & SPARKLING MINT LEMONADE

While the park offers the typical baseball fare, like hot dogs and peanuts, its food choices are heavily influenced by the area's Latino culture. Carne asada, fish tacos, and burritos are popular treats at the park.

FISH TACOS

PREP	COOK	MAKES
10 MINUTES	10 MINUTES	6 TACOS

	INGREDIENTS	
◇	1 pound	firm white fish, such as cod
◇		
◇	1 tablespoon	lime juice
◇	1 tablespoon	olive oil
◇	1 tablespoon	cumin
◇	1 teaspoon	salt
◇	¼ teaspoon	cayenne pepper
◇	6	flour tortillas
◇	optional toppings: chipotle mayo, sour cream, grated cheese, and lettuce	
◇		

1. Cut the fish into 2-inch cubes and place in a shallow baking dish.

2. In a small mixing bowl, combine the lime juice, olive oil, cumin, salt, and pepper. Whisk well and pour over the fish. Allow to marinate for 5 minutes.

3. In a skillet over medium heat, add the fish and marinade. Using tongs, carefully turn the pieces over after 3 minutes. Then cook another 3–4 minutes or until cooked through.

4. Evenly place fish on 6 tortillas, followed by chipotle mayo and desired garnishes. Serve immediately.

SOCAL KEEPS IT LOCAL

In 2015, the Natural Resources Defense Council and the Green Sports Alliance recognized the San Diego Padres as "Champions of Game Day Food." The accolades are well deserved. More than 95 percent of the concession stands and restaurants within Petco Park get their food from Southern California. Locally sourced foods greatly reduce transportation costs and waste but also increase food freshness within the park. Even baseball's greatest classics, like hot dogs, hamburgers, and nachos, come from local sources. The Padres also donate uneaten food to nearby shelters, create biofuels from cooking oils, and find other innovative practices to keep baseball — and its food — sustainable for years to come.

CHIPOTLE MAYO

PREP	COOK	MAKES
5	**0**	**1**
MINUTES	HOUR	CUP

INGREDIENTS

◇	1	chipotle pepper in adobo sauce
◇	1 teaspoon	adobo sauce
◇	1 teaspoon	lime juice
◇	1 cup	mayonnaise
◇	1 teaspoon	salt

1 Chop the pepper finely and place in a mixing bowl along with the adobo sauce, lime juice, mayonnaise, and salt. Stir to combine.

2 Serve on Fish Tacos. Store leftovers in an airtight container in refrigerator for up to 3 days.

SPARKLING MINT LEMONADE

PREP	COOK	MAKES
5	**1**	**2**
MINUTES	HOUR	QUARTS

INGREDIENTS

◇	1 quart	lemonade
◇	½ bunch	fresh mint leaves
◇	1 quart	sparkling water
◇		ice cubes
◇		

1 In a pitcher, combine the lemonade and fresh mint. Refrigerate for 1 hour.

2 Pour the sparkling water into the pitcher and stir to combine.

3 Serve in glasses with ice cubes.

AT&T PARK

LOCATION
San Francisco, California
OPENED
2000
CAPACITY
41,915
NICKNAMES
The Phone

In the spring of 2000, the San Francisco Giants opened their season in a new home. They moved from windy Candlestick Park, which they shared with the NFL's 49ers, to Pacific Bell Park. Later, AT&T bought the naming rights, and it is now known as AT&T Park. The Giants' new home has been good to both players and team alike. On August 7, 2007, slugger Barry Bonds belted his 756th home run to pass the great Hank Aaron as the all-time HR leader. A few years later, Matt Cain pitched a perfect game there on June 13, 2012. The team has also won three World Series titles (2010, 2012, and 2014) since the move.

CARIBBEAN RICE BOWL

with **PINEAPPLE SALSA** & **CRANBERRY-GINGER FIZZ**

AT&T Park sits on the edge of downtown San Francisco, along the water. Most seats curve around home plate and offer a spectacular view of San Francisco Bay. Being located in sunny California and near the water makes fruity drinks and seafood dishes a popular choice. But it's the Caribbean rice bowl, the Cha Cha Bowl, that is the fan favorite.

CARIBBEAN RICE BOWL

PREP	COOK	MAKES
10	**25**	**4**
MINUTES	MINUTES	BOWLS

INGREDIENTS

◇	1 cup	white rice
◇	1 tablespoon + 1 teaspoon	olive oil, divided
◇	2 cups	chicken broth
◇	1 teaspoon	crushed garlic
◇	1 teaspoon	turmeric
◇	1 pound	boneless chicken breasts
◇	1 teaspoon	cumin
◇	½ teaspoon	cayenne pepper
◇	½ teaspoon	allspice
◇	1 teaspoon	salt
◇	1 15-ounce can	black beans, drained
◇	8 ounces	frozen corn
◇	1	bell pepper
◇	1 recipe	pineapple salsa
◇	optional toppings: grated cheese, sour cream,	
◇	or guacamole (see page 65)	
◇		
◇		
◇		
◇		
◇		

1 In a saucepan, combine rice, 1 teaspoon olive oil, chicken broth, crushed garlic, and turmeric over medium heat. Bring to a simmer and cover. Cook for about 15 minutes or until the rice has absorbed all the liquid. Set aside.

2 Meanwhile, cut the chicken into bite-sized pieces and set aside.

3 In a mixing bowl, combine cumin, cayenne pepper, allspice, and salt. Add chicken and coat all sides.

4 In a skillet over medium-high heat, add 1 tablespoon olive oil. When the oil begins to smoke, carefully add the chicken and cook until no longer pink, about 10 minutes, stirring occasionally.

5 While the chicken cooks, heat the beans over low heat in a small saucepan.

6 Cook the corn according to package directions and set aside.

7 Chop the bell pepper into small pieces and set aside.

8 To assemble the bowl, place a heaping spoonful of rice in the bottom of the bowl. Add ¼ of the chicken, ¼ cup corn, ¼ cup beans, ¼ of the pepper, ¼ cup of pineapple salsa and desired garnishes. Serve hot.

PINEAPPLE SALSA

PREP	COOK	MAKES
15	0	1
MINUTES	MINUTES	CUP

	INGREDIENTS	
◇	½	pineapple
◇	1 recipe	pico de gallo (page 60)
◇	1 teaspoon	cumin
◇	1/8 teaspoon	cayenne pepper
◇	½ teaspoon	apple cider vinegar
◇	2 tablespoons	pineapple juice
◇		
◇		

1 Chop the pineapple into small pieces and add to mixing bowl.

2 Add pico de gallo, cumin, cayenne pepper, apple cider vinegar, and pineapple juice.

3 Stir well and serve on Caribbean Rice Bowl.

CRANBERRY-GINGER FIZZ

PREP	COOK	MAKES
5	0	2
MINUTES	MINUTES	QUARTS

	INGREDIENTS	
◇	1 quart	cranberry juice cocktail
◇	2 cups	ginger ale
◇	2 cups	lemonade
◇		ice cubes
◇		

1 In a pitcher, combine the cranberry juice, ginger ale, and lemonade. Stir well.

2 Serve in glasses with ice cubes.

Food Map

Take a culinary road trip right at home with diamond dishes from all thirty Major League ballparks!

American League

1. **BALTIMORE ORIOLES**
   Oriole Park at Camden Yards • Baltimore, Maryland
2. **BOSTON RED SOX**
   Fenway Park • Boston, Massachusetts
3. **CHICAGO WHITE SOX**
   U.S. Cellular Field • Chicago, Illinois
4. **CLEVELAND INDIANS**
   Progressive Field • Cleveland, Ohio
5. **DETROIT TIGERS**
   Comerica Park • Detroit, Michigan
6. **HOUSTON ASTROS**
   Minute Maid Park • Houston, Texas
7. **KANSAS CITY ROYALS**
   Kauffman Stadium • Kansas City, Missouri
8. **LOS ANGELES ANGELS OF ANAHEIM**
   Angel Stadium of Anaheim • Anaheim, California
9. **MINNESOTA TWINS**
   Target Field • Minneapolis, Minnesota
10. **NEW YORK YANKEES**
    Yankee Stadium • Bronx, New York
11. **OAKLAND ATHLETICS**
    O.co Coliseum • Oakland, California
12. **SEATTLE MARINERS**
    Safeco Field • Seattle, Washington
13. **TAMPA BAY RAYS**
    Tropicana Field • St. Petersburg, Florida
14. **TEXAS RANGERS**
    Globe Life Park in Arlington • Arlington, Texas
15. **TORONTO BLUE JAYS**
    Rogers Centre • Toronto, Ontario

National League

16. **ARIZONA DIAMONDBACKS**
    Chase Field • Phoenix, Arizona
17. **ATLANTA BRAVES**
    Turner Field • Atlanta, Georgia
18. **CHICAGO CUBS**
    Wrigley Field • Chicago, Illinois
19. **CINCINNATI REDS**
    Great American Ball Park • Cincinnati, Ohio
20. **COLORADO ROCKIES**
    Coors Field • Denver, Colorado
21. **LOS ANGELES DODGERS**
    Dodger Stadium • Los Angeles, California
22. **MIAMI MARLINS**
    Marlins Park • Miami, Florida
23. **MILWAUKEE BREWERS**
    Miller Park • Milwaukee, Wisconsin
24. **NEW YORK METS**
    Citi Field • Queens, New York
25. **PHILADELPHIA PHILLIES**
    Citizens Bank Park • Philadelphia, Pennsylvania
26. **PITTSBURGH PIRATES**
    PNC Park • Pittsburgh, Pennsylvania
27. **SAN DIEGO PADRES**
    Petco Park • San Diego, California
28. **SAN FRANCISCO GIANTS**
    AT&T Park • San Francisco, California
29. **ST. LOUIS CARDINALS**
    Busch Stadium • St. Louis, Missouri
30. **WASHINGTON NATIONALS**
    Nationals Park • Washington, DC

ONTARIO

NORTH DAKOTA

MINNESOTA

SOUTH DAKOTA

WISCONSIN

9

23

MICHIGAN

15

NEW YORK

MAINE

VERMONT
NEW HAMP

2

24

MASSACHUSETTS

10

RHODE ISLAND

CONNECTICUT

NEW JERSEY

DELAWARE

MARYLAND

NEBRASKA

IOWA

18

3

5

4

PENNSYLVANIA

25

OHIO

INDIANA

ILLINOIS

26

1

30

KANSAS

7

MISSOURI

29

WEST
VIRGINIA

VIRGINIA

19

OKLAHOMA

ARKANSAS

TENNESSEE

KENTUCKY

NORTH
CAROLINA

SOUTH
CAROLINA

TEXAS

MISSISSIPPI

ALABAMA

GEORGIA

17

LOUISIANA

14

6

FLORIDA

13

22

N

137

The ALL★FOOD Team

It's no wonder these real-life Major Leaguers performed at the plate — their food-related names make delicious dishes!

A★F

8
CHET LEMON
Chicago White Sox (1975–1981)
Detroit Tigers (1982–1990)

7
CHILI DAVIS
San Francisco Giants (1981–1987)
California Angels (1988–1990)
Minnesota Twins (1991–1992)
California Angels (1993–1996)
Kansas City Royals (1997)
New York Yankees (1998–1999)

9
DARRYL STRAWBERRY
New York Mets (1983–1990)
Los Angeles Dodgers (1991–1993)
San Francisco Giants (1994)
New York Yankees (1995–1999)

6

ALFREDO GRIFFIN
Cleveland Indians (1976–1978)
Toronto Blue Jays (1979–1984)
Oakland Athletics (1985–1987)
Los Angeles Dodgers (1988–1991)
Toronto Blue Jays (1992–1993)

4

COOKIE ROJAS
Cincinnati Reds (1962)
Philadelphia Phillies (1963–1969)
St. Louis Cardinals (1970)
Kansas City Royals (1970–1977)

5

PIE TRAYNOR
Pittsburgh Pirates
(1920–1935, 1937)

3

MIKE LAMB
Texas Rangers (2000–2003)
Houston Astros (2004–2007)
Minnesota Twins (2008)
Milwaukee Brewers (2008)
Florida Marlins (2010)

1

CATFISH HUNTER
Kansas City Athletics (1965–1967)
Oakland Athletics (1968–1974)
New York Yankees (1975–1979)

2

"PICKLES" DILLHOEFER
Chicago Cubs (1917)
Philadelphia Phillies (1918–1919)
St. Louis Cardinals (1920–1921)